HOW TO DESIGN A BOAT

—— John Teale ——

ADLARD COLES NAUTICAL
London

Second edition published by Adlard Coles Nautical 1998
an imprint of A & C Black (Publishers) Ltd
35 Bedford Row, London WC1R 4JH

First edition 1992
Reprinted 1996
Second edition 1998

ISBN 0-7136-4914-3

A CIP catalogue record for this book is available
from the British Library.

Set in 11/12pt Century, printed and bound in Great Britain by
J. W. Arrowsmith Ltd, Bristol

Contents

Contents

1 Preliminary sketches and calculations

Anyone having a reasonable eye for a fair curve and the merest smattering of mathematics can design a boat. The first effort may not be a world beater but, if built, should perform perfectly well and give a good deal of pleasure. What bothers most people having a go for the first time are the basics. How do I know how deep she will float? Where should I put the centreboard? What sort of area should the rudder be? And so on. In this book simple answers will be attempted to such questions while, by the end, the design process should have been taken far enough for the interested reader to be able to look at the published drawings of any type of craft, study them, and then, understanding what has gone on, use them as the basis for a design of their own.

Early on in the design process an approximate weight for the completed craft will need to be known, so some idea of how the boat is to be built will be required. Construction is a vast subject with much written about particular methods which, even so, leave many possibilities unexplored. In Chapter 6 some general structural guidelines are given, but the designer should really have a close look at examples of the type of build that interests him and learn from those. Imagine, while drawing, that you are going to build the vessel yourself and act accordingly.

Equipment

It takes a fair amount of gear to take a design to the stage at which the drawings can be presented to a builder with confidence, but the initial arrangement sketches require only:

- an ordinary clutch pencil with some HB leads and a drum sharpener
- some form of straight edge about 2–3 ft (600–900 mm) long
- a set square (clear plastic) with something like 8 in (200 mm) sides
- a really good pencil rubber
- a sheet of A1 cartridge paper
- a scale rule, either imperial or metric to suit your tastes, incorporating useful scales like $\frac{1}{2}$ in, $\frac{3}{4}$ in and 1 in = 1 ft (or 1 : 25, 1 : 15 and 1 : 10 metrically). It is quite hopeless trying to concoct some ingenious scale as, for instance, $3\frac{1}{2}$ mm = 1 in so as to be able to use a child's school ruler.

The longest French Curve that is available will also be useful occasionally, to harden up freehand sketches, supplemented by a smaller version with tighter curves. A drawing board is not strictly necessary at this stage – any table of convenient height will do. A drawing office supplies shop can provide all the gear mentioned. Additional equipment needed by the more ambitious will be described later.

The initial sketch

Now we'll have a go at drawing the initial sketches of the craft shown in Fig 1. This is a day sailer 20 ft (6 m) in length. Without

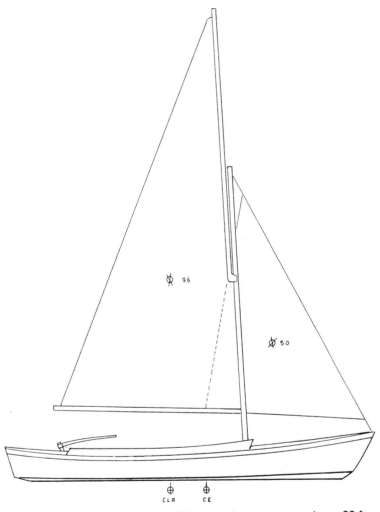

Fig 1   This is the boat that will be used as an example; a 20 ft (6 m) day sailer.

the rig and with a different layout she could equally well be an outboard powered vessel or even a motorboat with a low power inboard engine. The hull form would be the same in all cases. Don't worry about the meagre drawing tools you possess;

astonishingly accurate curves can be constructed freehand with patience and plentiful use of the rubber.

In what follows:

Loa is length overall, from stem to stern down the centreline not counting excrescences such as bowsprits and bumpkins.

Lwl is length on the waterline.

lwl (lower case first l) is load waterline – the waterline the boat is designed to float at.

Bwl is beam on the waterline.

D is the depth of the bottom of the main hull below the waterline at midships. It is not the same as draught, which is taken to the bottom of the keel at its deepest part.

All these are shown on Fig 2.

Looking at the above-water profile Fig 1, Lwl has turned out to be about 17 ft (5.2 m) because that gave what was considered a pleasing outline on an overall length of 20 ft (6 m).

Freeboard and sheer

Freeboard is the height of the deck edge above the water; typical freeboards at the bow are given in Fig 3. On a 17 ft Lwl, the freeboard at the bow is about 2.2 ft. Fig 2 also shows that freeboard at the stern is freeboard at the bow divided by 1.4, so here the figure would be $2.2 \div 1.4 = 1.6$ ft. The lowest part of the sheer curve occurs about two-thirds the overall length from the bow.

These freeboard recommendations are only guides, and many modern vessels have higher and less curvy deck edges. High freeboard brings unwelcome windage but makes for a marginally drier boat and adds something to stability by delaying the point where the deck edge goes under water. At that moment resistance to further heeling is suddenly reduced. A coaming adds freeboard, and being set back from the deck edge looks less high than topsides carried up to the same height. Reverse

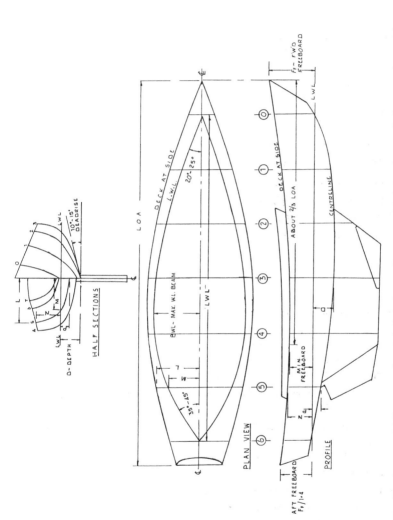

Fig 2 A round bilge version of the day sailer on which various of the terms used (such as Loa and waterline length) are shown.

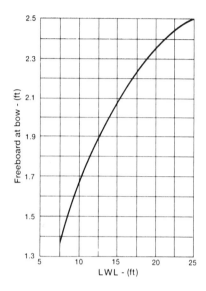

Fig 3   Suggested freeboard at the bow based on waterline length.

and S-shaped sheers can add height where it is needed (to give added hull depth in the way of accommodation, for instance) but are difficult to make attractive visually.

Convention has it that the bow is drawn facing to the right so that the starboard side is seen. This is the side on which the large oar or 'steerboard' was secured in the days before rudders were used. It is still traditionally the most important side of the boat in that starboard cabins and alleyways tend to be allocated to owners and officers.

Incidentally, don't be misled into thinking that a straight line sheer will look classy. It probably won't because, viewed from the side, the centreline of the boat at the bows (and to lesser extent at the stern) is further away from the eyes than is the middle of the vessel. This creates the optical illusion that the ends are drooping downwards. If the sheer is to look straight then some upward sweep of the deck edge is needed, particularly towards the bow.

The above-water profile drawing of Fig 1 can now be completed by adding the area below the lwl, but first we must estimate waterline beam.

Beam

Possible waterline beams (Bwl) based on waterline length are shown in Fig 4. In the example, waterline length (Lwl) is 17 ft (5.2 m) so Bwl is about 5.2 ft (1.6 m). Beam on deck is somewhere between 1.1 and 1.2 times waterline beam, so here maximum beam on deck would be between 5.7 ft (1.7 m) and 6.2 ft (1.9 m).

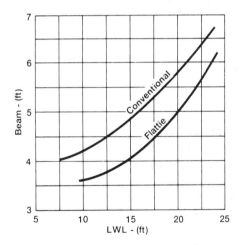

Fig 4 Suggested waterline beam at its maximum point based on waterline length. A flattie is a flat-bottomed boat whose recommended design features are further explored in Chapter 2.

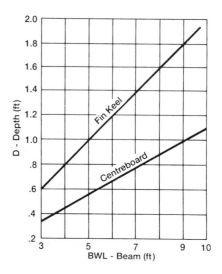

Fig 5   Approximate depth of hull below the waterline at midships for fin keelers and centreboarders. Based on waterline beam.

Depth

Another graph, Fig 5, shows the relationship between waterline beam and the depth of the main hull below the waterline at midships, D (Fig 2). A centreboarder will be a lighter boat than a fin keeler, so for a 5.2 ft waterline beam, a centreboarder's depth would be around 0.57 ft, while that of a fin keeler would be just over 1 ft.

There is another method of estimating depth of the main hull, D. This involves using what is known as the **block coefficient**, C_b. This is the ratio between the actual immersed volume of the hull to the product of waterline length, waterline beam and depth at midships. In other words, the ratio between the actual volume compared with the volume if it had been a box underwater, ie not shaped at all.

So, $C_b = \Delta \times 35/(L \times B \times D)$ where Δ is the weight of the hull in tons ie its displacement; but don't worry about the term displacement at the moment. It will be explained shortly and for the present can be considered as simply the weight of the boat completely fitted out and carrying its normal complement of crew, fuel, water, stores and so on. The multiplier, 35, converts tons to the equivalent volume in cubic feet of sea water (explanations later). L is waterline length, B is waterline beam and D is depth of hull at midships. Everything is measured in feet.

What we wanted from this potential calculation was D, so the formula can be re-written as: $D = \Delta \times 35/(L \times B \times C_b)$ and if the weight had been in pounds rather than tons we could put: $D = \Delta(\text{in lb})/(L \times B \times C_b \times 64)$.

What we still don't have is a number for C_b. An approximation (the actual figure will depend, of course, on how fine the underwater lines are) for hard chine forms is that $C_b = $ between 0.34 and 0.36. On round bilge types the figure will be a little lower, say $C_b = 0.32$.

So far we have been considering a 20 ft (6 m) day sailer. We don't know its weight at the moment, but a boatbuilder or friend might be able to estimate hull weight for you or you may be able to assess it yourself: see Chapter 2. To that figure you need to add crew weight, sails, spars, auxiliary, fuel, water and everything else you could carry aboard.

Suppose we chose a centreboard, hard chine version. A builder might estimate, say, 650 lb (292.5 kg) for the hull. To that you might add 400 lb (180 kg) for the other bits and pieces mentioned. The grand total is $650 + 400 = 1050$ lb (472 kg). Put that in the formula. We know L is 17 ft and B is 5.2 ft. $D = \Delta(\text{in lb})/(L \times B \times C_b \times 64)$ or, assuming C_b is 0.34, $D = 1050/(17 \times 5.2 \times 0.34 \times 64)$. That is, $D = 0.55$ ft. From Fig 5 showing D, a figure of 0.57 ft for D was found, so two differing schemes gave much the same result, which is encouraging! These D figures are pretty approximate but one has to start somewhere, and later on the results will be checked.

A fin keeler is presumed to have a ballast ratio of about 33 per cent. That is, if the overall weight including keel was 1800 lb and the fin keel itself weighed 600 lb the ballast ratio would be 600 ÷ 1800, or 0.33, which is 33 per cent.

So now we have sufficient ingredients for the first, rough, freehand sketches of the hull to be completed. Overall and waterline lengths are known, as are the figures for waterline and overall beam. The freeboard and sheer line have been decided upon and the depth of the hull below the water estimated.

Fig 6 shows a hard chine, centreboard version of the day sailer in Fig 1. We might as well begin with this hard chine type as being the easiest to design (and build).

First draw a straight line representing the waterline, lwl, in profile, and aim on drawing the sketch about 12 in (300 mm) long. This means suitable scales would be $\frac{1}{2}$ in = 1 ft or 1 : 25. At an appropriate distance below lwl and exactly parallel to it draw another straight line as the centreline of the plan view. A plan view is the shape of the boat looking down on it from above. Draw in the profile of the deck and then the keel or centreline. The depth of the hull at midships below the waterline is known, D, and on all slow-speed vessels like this one the transom bottom must be above the lwl to allow a smooth flow of water round the stern.

Now draw in the deck line in plan view. Maximum beam has been decided and we can assume on this version that it occurs at midships. At its aft end the deck might end in a transom, as shown, or come to a point and so create a double-ended craft. A double ender is slippery and seaworthy; a transom stern allows more space inside the boat and may permit a little more speed, especially on a reach or run or when under power. Too wide a transom can create problems in following seas when a big wave could lift the very buoyant, wide transom and in so doing force the bows deep into the water. This is the attitude a boat takes immediately before a broach, which is most unpleasant.

Having drawn the deck line in plan (and it should be slightly fuller over its stern half than forward, even with a double ender) divide the waterline length into an even number of equal spaces. In the example six divisions have been used and these are called stations. Since the boat is 17 ft (5.18 m) on the waterline, the

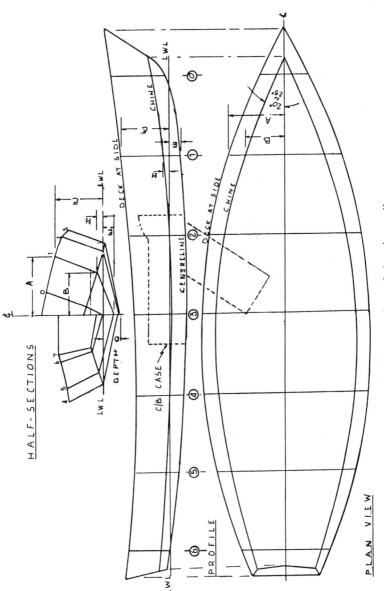

HALF-SECTIONS

PLAN VIEW

Fig 6   A first lines plan of a hard chine version of the day sailer.

11

stations are $17 \div 6 = 2$ ft 10 in (0.86 m) apart. Make sure the station lines are vertical and parallel to one another.

Next draw a half section at midships. This is a cross section through one side of the hull. The height and beam of the deck are known. From this point draw a line down through the beam on the waterline (also known). Then from the keel or centreline at the depth D and at an angle of between 10° and 15° put in the bottom line. Where this intersects the line down from the deck edge gives the height and width of the chine at midships. This point can be transferred to the profile and plan view outlines. Finally draw in the chine in plan and profile, roughly parallel to the deck and keel lines respectively, before sitting back to admire the result.

Fill in the other half-sections with those from stations 0–3 inclusive to the right of the centreline, and stations 4–6 inclusive to the left. Station 1 is drawn in detail on Fig 6. Dimensions A, B, C, E and H must correspond in all views.

Generally speaking a boat with a steeply vee'd bottom or rise of floor will heel more easily, but will knife along to windward more effectively than a flatter-floored rival. It will float a little deeper too, which helps windward performance, for there is no real substitute for depth of hull in the water to counteract leeway. Big rudders, centreplates and fins all help, of course, but are not the complete answer. Boats with shallower vee bottoms come into their own when reaching or running and under power. The rise of floor must increase as the bottom approaches the bow to reduce slamming in a head sea.

Looking at Fig 6 you may wonder why the shape of the load waterline (lwl) in plan view is not drawn in as it appears to have been with the round bilge version in Fig 2. It could have been, but its presence is not all that helpful on chine boats, and leads to problems in fairing which are best avoided at this stage.

All this probably seems a very mechanical way of drawing one particular type of boat, but there is no reason why this half-decker should not be transformed into a little cruising boat with the addition of a cuddy or what-have-you. It could equally well be a double ender of a totally different length and sheer line without making any difference to the design processes so far described.

As we continue, a system of checks will be used to validate what has been done in the initial stages and allow some freedom to amend. Here is the first of these checks.

We must now find the volume of the underwater area of the boat for reasons that will be explained in Chapter 2 and, at the same time, calculate the position of the fore and aft centre of area of the underwater volume. This centre is known as the **lcb** (longitudinal centre of buoyancy) and is determined by using multipliers, or levers, as shown in Tables 1 and 2. It's very straightforward.

Displacement calculation

The volume of displacement is found by working out the underwater area (below lwl) of each halfsection and then putting these figures into a table. Volume can then be translated into a weight, which should equal the weight of the boat – but more on this in Chapter 2.

On a hard chine boat areas can be calculated simply by dividing each half-section into rectangles and triangles as appropriate. Remember to measure areas on one side of the centreline only for each section.

The working of the calculation is straightforward and the example in Table 2 refers to the 20-footer. The Simpson Multipliers (SM) start at 1 on station 0 and continue as 4 and then 2 for as long as necessary. They end up as 4 and finally 1 again. Table 1 maps this out for various numbers of stations. The levers start at 0 on the midships station and then work outwards as 1, 2, 3 and so on as far as necessary. Finally the total of the half areas multiplied by Simpson Multipliers is itself multiplied by the common interval (the spacing between the stations) and then by 2/3. Common interval in this case is 2 ft 10 in or 2.83 ft (0.85 m). Although there was no area at station 6, the aft end

Preliminary sketches and calculations

Table 1 Layout of the displacement and lcb calculations for typical numbers of stations

Station	Area	SM	Product	Lever	Product
0		1		3	
1		4		2	
2		2		1	
3		4			Total
4		2		1	
5		4		2	
6		1		3	
			Total		Total

Station	Area	SM	Product	Lever	Product
0		1		4	
1		4		3	
2		2		2	
3		4		1	
4		2			Total
5		4		1	
6		2		2	
7		4		3	
8		1		4	
			Total		Total

Station	Area	SM	Product	Lever	Product
0		1		5	
1		4		4	
2		2		3	
3		4		2	
4		2		1	
5		4			Total
6		2		1	
7		4		2	
8		2		3	
9		4		4	
10		1		5	
			Total		Total

COAST
langley city hotel &
convention centre™

5	AREA	SM	Product	+
0	~~+~~	~~→ 14~~	~~4~~	Leon 3
1	4	12	48	2
2	2	19	38	1
3	4	28	108	3
4	2	25	~~100~~ 50	2
5	4	30	120	1
6	2	25	~~28~~ 50	3
7	4	17	68	2
8	2	10	20	1
9	4	5	20	
10	1	0		

~~1029~~
1052
~~527~~
522

Disp. 67328

Table 2 The displacement and lcb calculation for the hard chine version of the 20-footer when she was still in the freehand sketch stage

Common interval (station spacing) = 2.83 ft

Station	Area sq ft	SM	Product	Lever	Product
0	—	1	—	3	—
1	0.21	4	0.84	2	1.68
2	0.65	2	1.30	1	1.30
					2.98
3	0.84	4	3.36	—	
4	0.64	2	1.28	1	1.28
5	0.29	4	1.16	2	2.32
6	—	1	—	3	—
			7.94		3.60

Displacement in cu ft = 2/3 × 7.94 × 2.83 = 14.98
Displacement in lb = 14.98 × 64 = 958 lb in salt water
Longitudinal centre of buoyancy (lcb) = $\frac{3.6-2.98}{7.94}$ × 2.83 = 0.22 ft aft of midships

lcb should be a little way aft of midships, as it is here.

of the waterline length, in the case of a motor boat with an immersed transom there would have been.

The answer so far is in cubic feet. To translate this to a weight multiply by 64, because a cubic foot of sea water weighs 64 lb. If the answer had been in m³, multiply by 1025 for a figure in kg; a cubic metre of sea water weighs 1025 kg. A cubic foot of fresh water weighs 62.5 lb(1000 kg/m³).

Taking the lcb now, the results of multiplying by the levers are totalled – one total for forward of midships and another for aft. The smaller total is subtracted from the larger and this result is multiplied by the distance between the stations (the common interval) and divided by the volume total under the

Product column. The lcb should fall between 50 and 55 per cent of the waterline length aft of station 0.

Enough of these mathematical conundrums for the moment. Fuller explanations follow in subsequent chapters and we shall look at the round bilge fin keeler and a flattie version; and some possible areas for rudders, fin keels, centreboards and sails to complete the first sketches.

2 Completing the preliminary designs

In this chapter we shall look at displacement and the longitudinal centres of gravity and buoyancy (lcg and lcb). The initial sketches can then be fleshed out with the addition of the rudder, keel or centreboard, and sails.

Displacement

This is all to do with the Archimedes principle, which states that the weight of a floating body must be equal to the weight of the displaced fluid. In other words, if a boat was lowered gently into a tank brim-full of sea water, the weight of water that flowed over the edge of the tank would be exactly equal to the weight of the boat. The same would apply if the liquid were, say, mercury or petrol or fresh water. Its displaced weight would be the same as the boat's, though of course the *volume* of liquid to equal that weight would be different in each case. Very little mercury would be displaced (it weighs something like 750 lb/cu ft (12 075 kg/m^3) but, by comparison, quite a lot of petrol, which is lighter than sea water, would be displaced. Fresh water is lighter too, so it follows that since a greater volume will be displaced to equal the weight, a boat will float a little deeper in fresh water than in salt.

In the case of the 20-footer, its underwater volume, assuming it floats at the depth we estimated, is 14.98 cu ft (0.42 m^3) (see Table 2 in Chapter 1). Since sea water weighs 64 lb/cu ft (1025 kg/m^3) the weight of the displaced sea water must be 14.98 × 64 = 958 lb (434 kg) and that must also be the weight of the boat if it is to float at lwl.

So far, so good? The *real* weight of the boat is still an unknown, though it is hoped that it will be around 958 lb (431 kg) (the displacement to our desired waterline). We must now rectify that omission.

Table 3 gives weights for some typical boatbuilding materials. With the sheet products of steel, aluminium alloy and ply weight is given in lb/sq ft per millimetre of thickness and in kg/m^2 per millimetre of thickness. Thus, 3 mm steel weighs 3 × 1.6 = 4.8 lb sq ft (234 kg/m^2) while 9 mm ply comes out at 9 × 0.137 = 1.23 lb/sq ft (6.15 kg/m^2).

Table 3 Weights of boatbuilding materials

Material	Weight lb/cu ft (kg/m^3)	Weight lb/mm thick/sq ft (kg/mm thick/m^2)
Cedar	24 (385)	
African mahogany	32 (512)	
Douglas fir	33 (530)	
Larch	35 (560)	
Teak	41 (655)	
Oak (English)	45 (720)	
Cast iron	450 (7200)	
Lead	710 (11 400)	
Steel		1.6 (7.8)
Aluminium alloy		0.56 (2.73)
Plywood		0.137 (0.67)

Table 4 Preliminary weight calculation for a 20 ft day sailer

Item	Ply thickness mm	Weight/sq ft lb	Area sq ft	Weight lb
Bottom	9	1.2	81	97
Sides	9	1.2	64	77
Deck	6	0.83	25	20
Transom	12	1.65	5	8
Centreboard case	12	1.65	12	20
Centreboard	24	3.3	6	19
Rudder	24	3.3	5	17
Bulkheads	6	0.83	10	8
Total				266
Add two thirds				177
Total				443
Spars and sails				55
Coamings and floorboards				40
Thwarts and seats				25
Fittings				10
Crew				300
Grand total				873

The weight calculation for the 20-footer is shown in Table 4. All the ply structures are given an estimated area and thus weight. These are then totalled and in this case they come to 266 lb. Two thirds of that is then added in to allow for items of solid timber, such as chines, gunwales, keel, stringers, structural floors, frames and so on. So, 266 lb plus 177 lb is 433 lb, which represents the estimated weight of the bare hull. Add to this fitting-out and crew weights and we have a grand total of 873 lb.

This is near enough our hoped for 958 lb for work to proceed with some confidence. After all, there are still some weights we could add – what about an outboard plus fuel; an anchor and warp; and even a picnic basket? And the lines plan is still in its infancy, really. The boat may float a little high in the water at worst. If the numbers were wildly apart, however, measures would have to be taken to increase or decrease displacement as appropriate. Beam could, for instance, be increased or decreased; the keel line lifted or dropped; the chine line altered. None of these activities would have very much effect on structural weight but, done boldly, they could dramatically alter the displacement.

In this example two thirds of the sheet material weight was added to allow for the solid timber structure. Two thirds is an arbitrary but quite reasonable figure for conventional hard chine construction. However, with modern, lightweight structural methods where epoxy/glass connections are widely used and chines and gunwales may be of resin/glass lay-ups rather than solid timber, the figure of two thirds may be changed to one third. The latter is also appropriate when dealing with steel, aluminium alloy and even glassfibre, where the surface areas of hull, bulkheads and so forth are used as the basis.

On the other hand, in a really heavily framed chine boat, the solid timber may well weigh at least as much as the ply. Table 5 demonstrates this for a 14 ft 6 in by 6 ft 9 in (4.4 m × 2 m) cruising dinghy (Figs 7, 8 and 9). At the end, 10 per cent has been added to the grand total to allow for the many things that will have been forgotten!

Fig 8 shows a structural section for the boat which, incidentally, has a double bottom that drains into the rudder trunk. The crew sit on battened seats inside the vessel. Centreboard and rudder are not included on the timber list, since they are of GRP.

So, if in doubt about the weight ratio between sheet material and solid, do a rough calculation to set your mind at rest. With traditional timber construction always add up individual items and do not rely on ratios.

Table 6 shows the displacement calculation for the 14 ft 6 in (4.35 m) cruising dinghy in Fig 7. Displacement comes to 850 lb (382 kg), which compares quite well with the weight total of 603 lb (271 kg) before fitting out. As a matter of interest the block coefficient has been worked out – do you remember that from Chapter 1? Here it is 0.36, which falls in line with the predicted figure of between 0.34 and 0.36.

Table 5 Preliminary weight calculations for a 14 ft 6 in dinghy

Item	Scantling	Wt per ft or sq ft	Area sq ft	Weight lb
Ply				
Foredeck	6 mm	0.825 lb	6	5
Hull sides	6 mm	0.825	60	50
Hull bottom	6 mm	0.825	82	68
D'ble bottom	9 mm	1.24	66	83
Transom	9 mm	1.24	3	4
Centreboard case	9 mm	1.24	14	17
Rudder trunk	9 mm	1.24	4	5
Floors	9 mm	1.24	14	18
				250 lb
Longitudinals	*Inches*		*ft run*	
	$2\frac{1}{2} \times 1\frac{1}{4}$	0.73	126	92
	$1\frac{1}{4} \times 1$	0.30	36	11
	9×1	2.12	28	60
	4×1	0.94	28	26
	$4\frac{1}{2} \times 2$	2.12	17	36
				225 lb
Transverses	$2\frac{1}{2} \times 1\frac{1}{4}$	0.73	100	73 lb

Grand total = 250 + 225 + 73
= 548
Plus 10% = 603 lb

It was also suggested in Chapter 1 that the lcb be sited between 50 and 55 per cent of the waterline length aft of station 0. Here it is 55 per cent so all is well.

We have more calculations to do, however.

Longitudinal centre of gravity (lcg) and longitudinal centre of buoyancy (lcb)

Going back to the concept of the tankful of water in which a boat floats, suppose the water was frozen and the vessel lifted

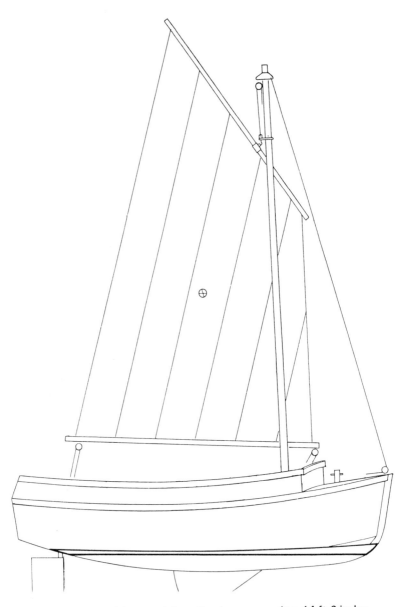

Fig 7   A balanced lug cruising dinghy measuring 14 ft 6 in by
6 ft 9 in (4.4 m by 2 m) with sail area 80 sq ft (7.4 m^2). The rudder
ships down through a trunk and the transom is cut away for a
long shaft outboard.

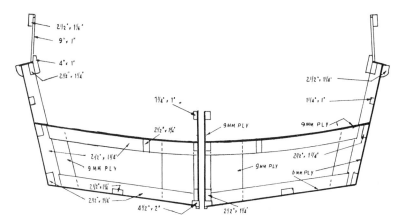

Fig 8   A scantling section through the cruising dinghy and used for the preliminary weight estimate.

out. There would now be a depression in the ice corresponding to the underwater shape of the boat. This must have a centre of area. After all, if the depression was used as a mould, and concrete was poured in and then lifted out after setting, it would have a balancing point. This point is known as the longitudinal centre of buoyancy (**lcb**) and the boat pivots about it in the water. The position of the lcb was calculated for the 20-footer in Table 2; it turned out to be 0.22 ft aft of midships. The underwater shape also has a vertical centre of area known as the vertical centre of buoyancy (**vcb**) at some distance below the waterline, but that is of no concern at the moment.

The longitudinal centre of all the weights connected with the boat (if the hull were balanced out of the water it would pivot about this point which is known as the longitudinal centre of gravity (**lcg**)) must now be found. For this we continue to use the recently completed weights calculation in Table 4. Table 7 sets out the calculations. For each of the weights previously used, a longitudinal centre of area or gravity position is estimated and written down as shown. Weights and their distance forward or aft of midships are then multiplied. The various figures are

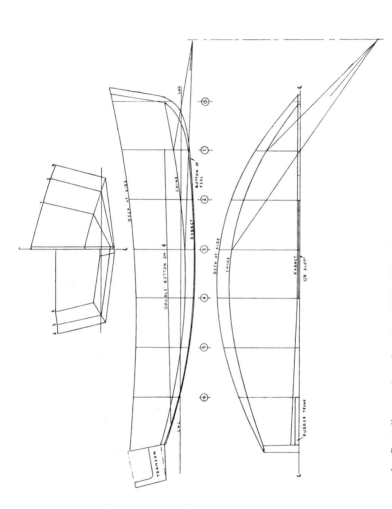

Fig 9 The rough, first lines plan for the 14 ft 6 in dinghy. The diagonal lines cutting through the forebody are generator lines for the conic projection and will be explained in Chapter 3.

Table 6 Displacement calculations for a 14 ft 6 in dinghy

Frame or station	Area sq ft	SM	Product	Lever	Product
0	—	1	—	3	—
1	0.14	4	0.56	2	1.12
2	0.58	2	1.16	1	<u>1.16</u>
3	1.06	4	4.24		<u>2.28</u>
4	1.10	2	2.20	1	2.20
5	0.45	4	1.80	2	3.60
6	—	1	—	3	—
			9.96		5.80

Displacement to Lwl. Frames at 2 ft centres
Scale 1 in = 1 ft

Displacement $= \frac{2}{3} \times 9.96$ ft $\times 2 \times 64$
     $= 850$ lb

Block coefficient $(C_b) = \frac{850}{12 \times 5.75 \times 0.54 \times 64}$
     $= 0.36$

Longitudinal centre of buoyancy (lcb) $= \frac{(5.8 - 2.28)}{9.96} \times 2$
     $= 0.7$ ft aft station 3

If lcb is 0.7 ft aft of station 3, it is 6.7 ft aft of station 0 (stations are at 2 ft centres). Thus the lcb is:

lcb $= \frac{6.7}{12} \times 100$
     $= 55$ per cent of waterline length aft of station 0
     (waterline length is 12 ft)

totalled; a spot of subtraction and division follows; and soon enough, an lcg figure appears. This turns out to be 0.6 ft aft of midships.

The distance between the lcb (Table 2) and lcg (Table 7) positions is small (0.38 ft) and not worth bothering about, although the consequences of a wide gap between the two centres is shown in Fig 10. The boat will trim until the new lcb (new, because trimming has altered the underwater hull shape) is in line with the lcg.

On a boat like this one where crew weight is a significant and movable factor, and where unthought-of items creep aboard

Table 7 Calculation for lcg on a 20 ft day sailer

Item	Weight lb	Lcg from midships ft Forward	Lcg from midships ft Aft	Moment lb ft Fwd	Moment lb ft Aft
Bottom	97	—	—	—	—
Sides	77	—	—	—	—
Deck	20	2.0		40	
Transom	8		9.25		74
Centreboard case	20	1.25		25	
Centreboard	19	1.25		24	
Rudder	17		10.00		170
Bulkheads	8		1.5		12
Totals	266			89	256

Lcg so far is $\frac{256-89}{266}$ = 0.65 ft aft of midships
Use this information for the next item

Two thirds ply hull	177		0.65		115
Sails and spars	55	3.25		179	
Coamings, floorboards	40		1.0		40
Thwarts, seats	25		4.0		100
Fittings	10	—	—	—	—
Crew	300		1.0		300
Grand total	873			268	811

Final lcg is $\frac{811-268}{873}$ = 0.6 ft aft midships

Where a dash occurs in the lcg or Moments columns it has been assumed that the lcg is at midships. (A **moment** is a weight × a distance.)

to be stowed randomly, a limited amount of trim adjustment can be made when the boat is afloat. However, to achieve a level trim with only the weights considered, either some weight will have to be added forward or the hull lines fined forward and filled aft to bring the lcb aft and under the lcg. This could probably be most easily achieved by lowering the chine line towards the stern while lifting it forward. After such alterations, check that the displacement is still what is required and that all fore and aft lines are still sweet and fair.

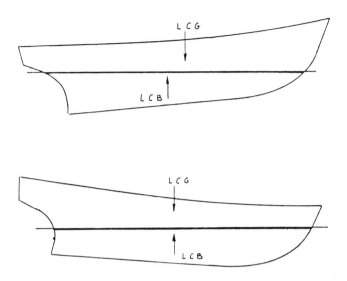

Fig 10   If the lcb and lcg are not in line the boat will trim until they are.

In practice the lcg of the bare hull nearly always ends up near midships and it is with the fitting-out items that adjustments are made. Thus, moving an engine and/or its batteries can alter the lcg quite a bit. Maybe anchor chain can be stowed somewhere other than in a chain locker right forward. Gas bottles can perhaps be sited where they can usefully contribute to the balancing act. As a last resort a small amount of inside ballast could do the trick. Whatever the temptation, do not use items like fuel and water to help sort out a recalcitrant lcg. These should be sited as near the lcb as possible, so that their constantly altering weight does not play too much havoc with the trim. In the lcg calculation their tank weight in half-full condition should be included, and the sums for moments done as with all the other items.

That more or less concludes the calculation side of things, at least as far as the preliminary drawings are concerned.

Other tonnages

Various other tonnages, Registered, Thames and Deadweight, are used when describing ships and (often incorrectly) yachts.

Registered tonnage is the figure that is carved into the main beam of a yacht or otherwise permanently and prominently displayed. Despite the name, it is not a weight at all but an assessment made by the DoT (or someone acting on their behalf as is often the case with yachts) of the internal volume of the vessel. If the volume is in cu ft it is divided by 100 and called tons. If in m^3 it is divided by 2.83 to arrive at the same answer.

When measuring for volume there are certain exempted spaces, such as double bottoms to carry water ballast, which are not measured. This first answer is called the gross tonnage, and from it may be deducted areas such as engine and chart rooms, crew's quarters, and so forth to give register or net tonnage.

The word 'tons' used in this context may derive from the fact that cargo vessels were once assessed on the numbers of casks or 'tuns' of wine they could carry. Harbour dues are traditionally paid on net tonnage, while passenger ship tonnages in promotion blurbs are normally gross. The 50 000 ton *Extravaganza* implies that she is 50 000 tons gross.

Cargo ships, bulk carriers, tankers and the like are usually quoted as being so many tons deadweight (dwt). Deadweight is the weight in tons that a ship can carry when loaded to the maximum permissible draught. Deadweight includes not only cargo but also movable stores, such as provisions, fuel and fresh water. What a ship weighs when completely empty is termed Lightship and therefore Lightship + Deadweight = Load displacement.

Thames Measurement (TM) or Thames Tonnage is:

$$TM = \frac{(L - B) \times B \times \frac{1}{2}B}{94}$$

where L = length and B = beam or, more simply:

$$TM = \frac{(L - B) \times B^2}{188}$$

Until the 1850s this was the tonnage measurement for cargo ships and also the rating measurement for yacht racing. In that form and several minor variations it continued for many years after merchant vessels had adopted a more sensible measurement. Indeed it was often used when describing yachts right up until the Second World War, though not then as a racing rating.

Its drawback is clear. Beam is heavily penalised while the depth of hull and sail area are ignored. Consequently racing yachts were built with ludicrously narrow hulls and, to compensate for the inevitable loss of stability and sail-carrying ability, great draught and enormously heavy ballast keels. These were the notorious British 'plank-on-edge' yachts described by the great Scottish designer G L Watson as approaching Euclid's definition of a line as having length but no breadth. An Essex agricultural implement maker, E H Bentall, designed and built the phenomenally successful 110 ft (33.5 m) yawl *Jullanar* with a length/beam ratio of 6 : 1 (today's figure would be more like 4 : 1) and then proceeded to build a 10-tonner (TM) called *Evolution*, shown in Fig 11. On a waterline length of 50.75 ft (15.2 m) her beam was 6.5 ft (2 m), a length/beam ratio

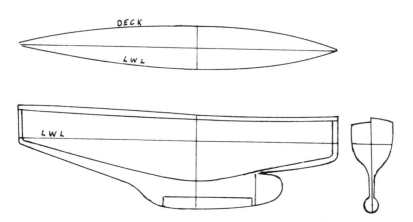

Fig 11   Lines of *Evolution*, an extreme example of the plank-on-edge type of British yacht of the late 1800s. She was actually built in 1880.

of 7.8. Though she was not a success, having stability problems, it shows how far people were prepared to go to fit in with the rating rules of the day.

Hull form

So far we have concentrated on the hard chine version of the day sailer but there are two variants: the flattie shown in Fig 12 and the round bilge version in Fig 13 which first appeared as Fig 2.

Water pushed aside by a boat as it moves through the water is forced downwards as well as sideways. As a consequence its average direction of flow is diagonally downwards and from bow to stern. Water, disturbed from a free run by angles (such as the chines), eddies and becomes turbulent, absorbing power in doing so. Thus the gentler the curves it has to flow along the happier it will be, with the consequence that a round bottom hull will be slightly easier to drive through the water than a chine rival, especially at the velocities at which sailing craft and low speed motor boats commonly travel.

As knots increase the hard chine or vee bottom hull starts to come into its own. Then the water rushing along the bottom and bearing on a surface slightly angled down into its flow (nearly all boats trim by the stern as speeds rise) will have a lift component. That is, it will try to lift the stern, reducing the area of hull in the water and thus the power requirement to drive it. The water will lift a flattish surface more easily than a curved one round which the water will tend to flow rather than push. So a chine form is good for high planing speeds on a sailing vessel and most of the time on a motor boat. It is seaworthy, easier to build than round bottom and unjustly mocked by those who are convinced by the arguments of GRP boatbuilders (glassfibre needs plenty of built-in curves to overcome its inherent floppiness).

There is, of course, more to hull form than simply deciding between chine and round bilge configurations and then aiming for a smooth flow of water round the hull by drawing fair lines. There is, for instance, a matter of how the displacement is to be spread through the length. In other words, should a lot of the underwater volume be concentrated around the middle of the vessel leading to fine, low volume ends, or would full sections towards bow and stern be preferable? The answer is that it mostly depends on the projected speed of the boat. Chapter 5 deals with the subject in more detail, but in the meantime if lines plans shown in this book are used as examples, all should be well. Select the lines of craft which are to perform similar tasks to the one you are sketching.

Power, whether provided by sails or an engine, is used up by making waves as the boat pushes through the water, and in overcoming the friction between hull and water. Methods of reducing the first loss are covered in Chapter 5 dealing with the distribution of displacement. Frictional losses are reduced by cutting down on the area of hull in contact with the water. Hence a fin keel will cause less frictional resistance than a full length keel, and a centreboard, when raised, will create less resistance than either. Thus, if speed is of the essence on, say, a sailing yacht, a fin keel is probably the right choice, though the craft will probably be less steady on the helm than a long-keeler and so may not make such a good cruising yacht.

A centreboard, though splendid in reducing wetted area, is difficult to combine with effective (and thus low slung) outside ballast. It can be operated with its slot set in a shallow ballast keel, but the presence of the keel means that some of the potential low wetted area advantages of the centreboard are lost. A bulb of lead or iron may be incorporated at the bottom of the board so that it acts low down when lowered and nestles in a recess formed in the hull in the 'up' position. The board, in such a case, normally operates by sliding vertically down the case, like a dagger board, rather than pivoting. This is an effective scheme, usually called a lifting keel, but the lifting arrangements tend to be rather costly and complicated, while the whole

Fig 12   A 21 ft (6.4 m) flattie with
plumb sides and parallel-sided
transoms fore and aft. It is easier
to build a transom than a stem
and, provided it is kept well
clear of the water, there is no
loss of sea-keeping ability.
Though a sectional view
or body plan has been
drawn, there is actually
no need for this on such
a simple boat.

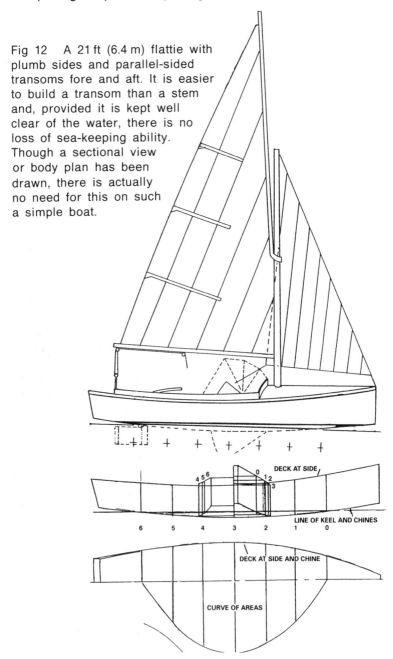

thing may not be as structurally sound as a true, integral ballast keel. Let us return to the task of settling on a hull form.

Flatties

Though rarely seen in this country, flat-bottom vessels are relatively popular in other parts of the world; particularly in America where they are used for small commercial craft as well as dinghies and yachts. Provided they are sensibly designed, they can have a good performance and give a lot of pleasure afloat. And because they are easy to build, particularly the plumb-sided types, they are well worth considering for the first design and build exercise.

Being of box shape, a flattie will float higher in the water than any other hull form and consequently must be reasonably narrow to ensure that an adequate depth of hull is immersed. Failing this, the boat will tend to skitter about on the surface of the water and be a pig to handle. Over-size centreboards and rudders are a feature of virtually all flatties but even these cannot make up entirely for a lack of immersed hull. Beam, therefore, should be kept down to ensure a length/beam ratio of not less than about 3.5:1. Fig 4 sets out some recommended beams.

Flatties may be plumb-sided for maximum initial stability and internal volume, or with flared sides for greater reserve stability and possibly a more forgiving nature. Fig 12 shows a lines plan of a 21 ft (6.4 m) plumb-sided type. It could not be easier to draw with the deck and chine lines coinciding (except possibly, at bow and stern) in plan view; and keel and chine lines coinciding in profile.

Flat-bottom boats need careful and experienced handling offshore particularly the unballasted types, and on this score it is worth mentioning that an outside ballast keel can be constructed with ease. However, sail area should always be on the modest side and the boat should be designed with commensurably modest freeboard to reduce windage.

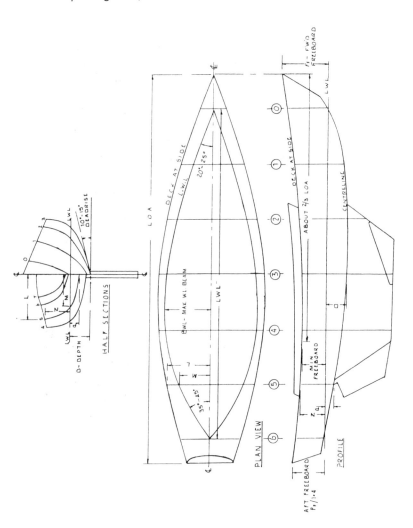

Fig 13 The basic lines plan in round bilge form.

Round bilges

Fig 13 shows the 20 ft (6 m) day sailer in round bilge form.
First draw the deck/sheerline and the keel/centreline in profile

using the suggested depth (D) measurement for a 5.2 ft (1.5 m) waterline beam fin keeler (just over 1 ft (300 mm)) as in Fig 5. Next draw the waterline (lwl) and deck line in plan view. The maximum waterline beam normally occurs a little way aft of midships, as shown. The curve should be somewhat fuller aft than forward. Then sketch in the sections, preferably starting with those occurring at stations 1, 3 and 5. When you are satisfied with those, draw in the remainder. Dimensions L, M, N and P, shown on the half-section at station 5, must correspond in all views with similar rules applying to the remainder of the half-sections.

If the sections are barrel-shaped the boat will tend to roll like a barrel so make them straightish over a portion of their underwater area.

Fin keels

From Fig 14 it looks as if the possible area of fin keel for a boat 17 ft on the waterline might be about 17 sq ft (1.6 m^2). This is a fairly large affair, as can be seen, and is not to be confused with the minimum-area keels as used on Flying Fifteens, for instance. Which only goes to show that there are no hard and fast rules! Draw in what pleases you and keep the lower, forward tip of the keel just aft of the mast centreline.

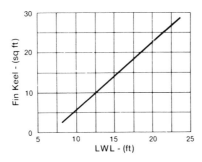

Fig 14 Suggested area of fin keel based on waterline length.

Whatever the shape and area of a fin keel, eventually its longitudinal centre of gravity (lcg) will need to be determined so that the lcg of the boat as a whole lies in the same line as the lcb. Taking the round bilge 20 footer as an example, a quick estimate of the displacement from the half-sections suggested that it was about 1500 lb (675 kg) with the lcb 0.22 ft aft of midships. Previously the weight of the centreboard chine version had been calculated as 873 lb (393 kg). On a fin keel round bilge version scantlings would probably be beefed up somewhat. There would, for instance, need to be heavier structural floors to carry the keel bolts and the hull thickness might well be increased to 12 mm. Anyway, assume that weight, without fin, increases by 150 lb from 873 to 1023 lb (460 kg), but that the lcg stays at its original positioning, 0.6 ft aft of midships.

For the juggling we are about to do it will be easiest if distances are measured from station 0. Thus the lcg location of the hull 0.6 ft aft of midships is 3×2 ft 10 in (the station spacing) plus 0.6 ft aft of station 0. That is $8.5 + 0.6 = 9.1$ ft.

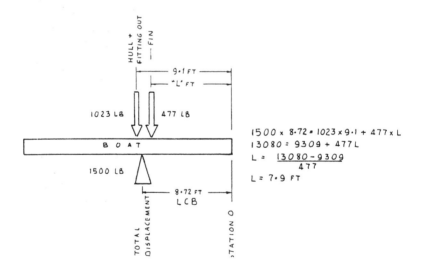

Fig 15 Working out the required position of fin keel and ballast.

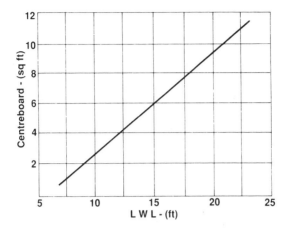

Fig 16 Centreboard area using waterline length as a guide.

The lcb of the fin keeler is 0.22 ft aft of midships or 8.72 ft aft of station 0. Total weight required is around 1500 lb (675 kg), so if the boat is 1023 lb then the fin, including ballast, must weigh 1500 − 1023 = 477 lb (214 kg) (ballast ratio, 32 per cent).

Fig 15 shows the calculation for the lcg of the fin keel, with the result that its lcg should be 7.9 ft aft of station 0.

Centreboards

Suggested areas are given in Fig 16 based on waterline length. Here waterline length is 17 ft, so the plate area would be about 7.3 sq ft (0.68 m^2). The bottom, forward tip of the centreboard when lowered should be a little aft of the mast centreline.

Rudders

Fig 17 shows suggested areas based on lateral plane area. The latter is the area of the underwater profile view; in this case

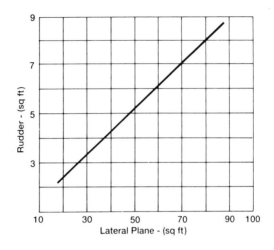

Fig 17   Rudder area based on lateral plane area. The latter is the underwater profile area of the vessel.

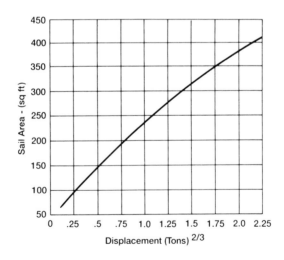

Fig 18   Sail area based on displacement tons.

about 29 sq ft (2.7 m^2). Rudder area would therefore be about 3.2 sq ft (0.3 m^2).

Sail area

Fig 18 explains these calculations. Sail areas are based on displacement in tons raised to the power of 2/3. This means that the figure for displacement in tons is first squared and then the cube root of that number found. If the displacement of the fin keeler is 1500 lb, that is $1500 \div 2240 = 0.67$ tons. Square 0.67 and the answer is 0.45; the cube root of that is 0.77 and so the sail area would be about 180 sq ft. For the centreboard version of 873 lb (0.39 tons) desirable sail area appears to be about 150 sq ft.

As to distribution of area, on sloop rigs the mainsail commonly has about twice the area of the jib, while on cutters the combined areas of the two headsails tend to be about 70 per cent of that of the main. Thus, on a total area of 180 sq ft the headsails would have a combined area of 75 sq ft and the main, 105 sq ft.

The initial sketches of the boat have now been taken as far as they can. Estimates have been checked and all is now ready for the task of drawing plans accurately. This will take more equipment than has been used so far and in the next chapter suggestions will be made in that direction. Proper lines plans of the day sailer in hard chine and round bilge forms with faired-in keel versions will be shown.

3 Making the working drawings

So far the dreamed-of boat has been sketched in some detail, but only freehand, and though these drawings would form the basis of a design, they are not enough to present to a boatbuilder – unless he happened to be knowledgeable, imaginative, courageous and possibly in need of work. To convert these sketches into useful plans will require quite a bit more drawing gear. But we will assume that the diligent reader will want to soldier on, so here goes.

Drawing board

Though it would be possible to complete the drawings on sheets of paper laid on the dining room table, that would be a tedious undertaking. To make the job bearable a proper drawing board with a parallel motion system, or something similar, is almost a necessity. Such things can be had with simple stands allowing them to be used flat on a table. Upright, engineer's boards and stands are not much use in boat work. The minimum, useful size for a board is A1 and drawing paper can be stuck to it with masking or draughting tape.

Splines

For drawing long curves, flexible plastic battens are used, called splines. These are about 4 ft (1.2 m) in length. They can be had parallel-sided or tapered. The latter are useful since a tighter curve can be drawn with the thinner end than with a normal, parallel-sided spline. So if money is no object one of each is ideal. Battens can also be home-hewn from Perspex. Using 2 mm Perspex sheet, cut a smoothly finished strip about $\frac{1}{4}$ in (6 mm) wide. Splines can be used flat or on edge.

Weights

To hold the battens in place lead weights are used (Fig 19). They weigh about 4 lb (1.8 kg) each and six are plenty. The

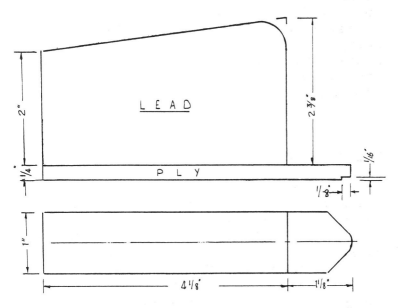

Fig 19   A typical lead weight used in conjunction with splines.

notched plywood base holds the spline down. Weights can be bought complete or made at home by those with casting skills. Home-made ones need painting before use or fingers will rapidly become filthy.

Curves

In some places, such as the sections of a round bottom boat (and below the chine in some hard chine forms), the forward part of buttocks, and the aft length of some waterlines, the curve may be too hard for a spline. In these areas, then, what are known as ship's curves are used. These are of clear plastic and vary in shape from very gentle curves to quite steep ones. Unhappily they are often sold in boxes of 20 or 40 and most of them will be quite useless for yacht work. If it can be arranged, buy two small curves very rounded at one end; one big ramshorn (its shape is as implied); and a couple of long curves which start out gently but finish in bold sweeps (Fig 20).

Fig 20   Five useful ship's curves. The longest are about 2 ft (0.6 m) in length.

Planimeter

This is for measuring area and is used mainly on displacement calculations. Planimeters can be had with variable or fixed scales. The latter are less expensive but still by no means cheap. Fixed scale answers can be converted into the answer in any other scale. If a planimeter measured only in a 1 in scale and the drawing had been done to a $\frac{3}{4}$ in scale, multiply the 1 in scale answer by the square of the inverted actual scale. That is, in the case of a $\frac{3}{4}$ in scale by $4^2/3^2$ or 16/9. If the used scale had been 1/2 in the multiplier would have been 4/1, and so on.

If in doubt, draw a shape of known area (perhaps a square or circle) to the scale you are working on; go round it with the planimeter and find out what the multiplier should be for it to give the right answer. Measure the area two or three times just as a check.

As remarked, planimeters are expensive (though it is possible to pick them up second-hand) and the first and perhaps only-time designer might prefer the infinitely cheaper expedient of using squared transparent paper. This can be had in a variety of scales, both imperial and metric. The idea is to lay the paper over the area to be measured and then count the squares. Make sure this transparent paper can be had in the scale you will need before starting drawing. If not, change the scale! It's a tedious job, though accurate enough for practical purposes.

Of course areas can be divided into rectangles and triangles and then calculated, but squared paper will be quicker and probably more accurate.

Sundries

Though most drawing work will still be done with HB leads, harder H leads may also be handy on occasion. For the grid of a lines plan (of which more in due course) fine ink lines are preferable and are achieved with a cartridge pen, such as the

0.25 Rotring. Pencil drawings do not reproduce very well by the normal dyeline process and need to be inked in, or traced in ink. For this work a thicker pen, such as an 0.4 Rotring, will complement the 0.25.

Sometimes circles or bits of circles need to be drawn. A pair of pencil and ink bows are then necessary, plus, maybe, pencil and ink compasses.

For erasing ink blots and runs (and in all probability there will be some) you can use a sharp scalpel, but you will need to go over the scraped part with a rubber to smooth the surface before having another go with ink.

Now the gear is assembled it is time to start drawing again, starting with a proper lines plan. The freehand sketch already completed is used as a reference. The new lines plan should be drawn to a scale so that it ends up roughly 30 in (0.76 m) long. Much bigger than that and it will be difficult to see everything from bow to stern in one glance and anyway it may not fit on the drawing board. Much smaller and it will be hard to achieve sufficient accuracy.

Just before getting down to detail there is one matter that should be discussed.

Rabbet (or rebate) line

On the rough lines plans so far drawn everything came to a point on the centreline: deck, stem, keel, the lot. But when you consider actual constructional arrangements this can't always be right. On a steel or alloy vessel, the sides and bottom at the centreline are likely to be connected via a stem/keel bar. Since, on a boat of our size, that bar would probably be only 3/8 in(9 mm) thick and its half-breadth to each side of the centreline only 3/16 in (4.5 mm) it is probably accurate enough to assume all endings are on the centreline. But on a GRP boat, for instance, space would have to be made for laminators to lay glass and resin on the inner faces of stem and keel. They couldn't do this properly, especially at the stem, if everything came to a point. So the forward and keel endings would have to have a radius on the centreline.

In the case of a timber-built craft the planking has to be fastened into solid wood at stem and keel and this must be stout enough to accept fastenings and allow an adequate landing between planking and stem or keel. This landing is known as faying surface, and its breadth should be at least twice the thickness of the planking. On ply construction the faying surface should be even broader than that.

The designer sketches out stem and forefoot planking endings to decide on a suitable rabbet line width (Fig 21). Lines plans are usually drawn to the outside of planking and so the width of the rabbet line governs the half-breadth of all endings on the centreline.

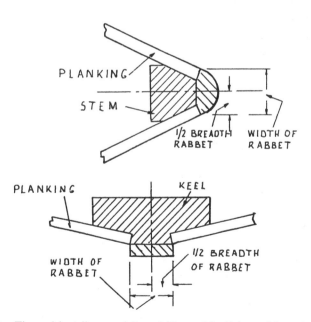

Fig 21 The rabbet line and its width and half-breadth at keel and stem.

At the keel, other considerations also apply. On this day sailer there is either a fin keel or a centreboard and centreboard case. The keel member must be wide enough to accept these and this governs the width of the rabbet line in that area (see Fig 21 again). On this 20-footer the rabbet width might be 5 in (125 mm) in the area of the keel or centreboard, tapering to $2\frac{1}{2}$ in (65 mm) at stem and stern. Half-breadths seen on the lines plan would be half those figures, of course. The rabbet line should be straight in profile where a fin is to be bolted on.

On steel and alloy craft a box fin keel would normally be used welded to the completed shell, so keel rabbet line widths would not apply. On a GRP boat, the fin keel might well be faired into and be integral with the shell to give a shape rather similar to that shown on the round bilge lines plan which follows. Alternatively, the fin could be a heavy metal plate bolted on to the shell.

Canoe stern, round bilge version

Just to show another possibility, Fig 22 demonstrates a canoe stern variant of the half-decker with the fin keel integral with the hull. To ring the changes further, construction is assumed to be traditional wood, not ply, with steamed timbers and mahogany carvel planking. This sort of thing usually turns out to be at least twice as heavy as ply building, with obvious consequences on the depth of the hull below the waterline at midships, D.

It would therefore be advisable to have a go at another weight calculation and Table 8 shows the way. The result appears to be that the hull weight has risen from 443 lb (200 kg) for the ply, centreboard type, Table 4, to a formidable 953 lb (440 kg) for this version and the overall displacement from 785 lb (356 kg) to 1853 lb (840 kg). The weight calculation should be extended to take in fore and aft centres of gravity and moments, as it did in Chapter 2, to produce an LCG position.

Canoe stern, round bilge version

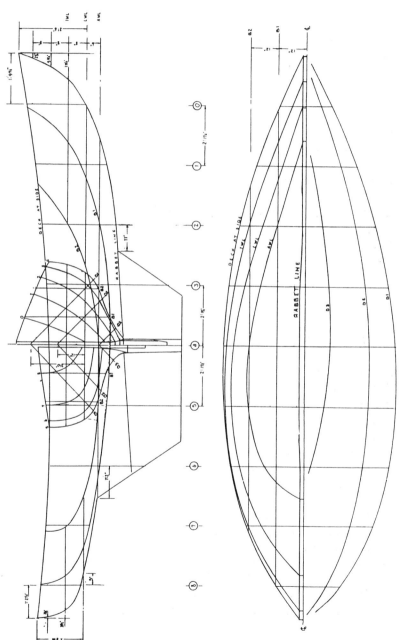

Fig 22   The round bilge, canoe stern version of the day sailer.

Table 8 Weight calculations for a 20 ft day sailer in round bilge and traditional timber construction form

Item	Material	Scantling	Wt/sq. ft or ft run	Length or area	Weight lb
Shell	Mahog	5/8 in	1.66 lb	150 sq ft	250
Deck	Mahog	5/8 in	1.66 lb	25 sq ft	42
Rudder	Mahog	3/4 in	1.95 lb	9 sq ft	17
Fin keel	Mahog	5 in	13.3 lb	17 sq ft	226
Timbers	E Oak	$1\frac{1}{4} \times 1$ in	0.4 lb	140 ft	56
Stem	E Oak	3×3 in	2.8 lb	10 ft	28
Keel	E Oak	$7 \times 2\frac{1}{2}$ in	5.46 lb	8 ft	44
Stern post	E Oak	3×3 in	2.8 lb	10 ft	28
Floors	E Oak	2×2 in	1.25 lb	8 ft	10
Deck beams	E Oak	$1\frac{1}{4} \times 1\frac{1}{4}$ in	0.5 lb	18 ft	9
Knees	E Oak				45
Beam shelf	Or pine	$3 \times 1\frac{1}{2}$ in	1.03 lb	42 ft	43
Stringer	Or pine	$2\frac{1}{2} \times 1\frac{1}{2}$ in	0.95 lb	33 ft	28
Bulkheads	Ply	$\frac{1}{2}$ in	1.5 lb	10 sq ft	15
Angle floors	Steel	$30 \times 30 \times 3$	1.0 lb	25 ft	25
					866
				+10%	87
				Hull weight in lb=	953
				+Fitting out and crew weight	450
					1403
				+Ballast keel at, say,	450
				Displacement in lb=	1853

A glance at this weight calculation will show that after the first total of 866 lb, 10 per cent was added. This was to allow for fastening, paint and things that had been forgotten: The item 'knees' was left pretty vague and the figure of 45 lb is simply a guess at a total for stem and stern knees, hanging and lodging knees, a couple of breasthooks and so forth. The construction plan hasn't been drawn at this stage so everything is pretty much guesswork.

Back to the depth of hull below water at midships. This, in Chapter 1, was estimated at a little over 1 ft (300 mm) for a fin keeler of modern construction. Now, in the light of that latest weight calculation, we had better increase that figure somewhat, guessing it to be 1 ft 4 in (400 mm), taken from lwl to the rabbet line at midships. Bearing that figure in mind, elbows can be squared and work on a new, bigger lines plan contemplated. The first, freehand round bilge lines plan can be modified to take in the new D figure, the canoe stern and the reverse tuck to the garboards.

Grid

The basis for all lines plan is an accurate grid which shows waterlines, buttocks (in their straight line views), centrelines, stations and the slope of the diagonals. This grid is usually drawn in ink on cartridge paper which doesn't expand and contract as much as tracing paper. Depending on the size of the drawing board a suitable scale for this 20-footer might be 1 in = 1 ft (1:12) or, more accurately, $1\frac{1}{2}$in = 1 ft (1:8). On a metric scale 1:10 would seem a good compromise. Nine stations would suffice here with stations 0 and 8 at the ends of lwl. When drawing a grid, be super-accurate. Measure and re-measure. Make sure that lines are really parallel or at right angles, as appropriate.

Waterlines

These are horizontal slices through the hull, parallel to the waterline (lwl) at which it is hoped the boat will float. A waterline appears as a straight line in profile and in section and as a curve in plan. Half-breadths from centreline must agree in sectional and plan views. Three waterlines are drawn here: lwl, Lwl and Awl.

Buttocks

These are vertical slices through the hull parallel to the centre-line. They show up as straight lines on plan and sectional views and as curves in profile. They are marked B1 and B2 in Fig 22. A buttock's height above or below lwl must be the same on profile and sectional views and the point where a buttock cuts a waterline must be on the same vertical line in profile and plan views. Fig 23 shows this.

Diagonals

When drawing the sections on a plan of a round bilge boat it will become apparent that parts of their shape are not very well defined by either waterlines or buttocks. Here diagonals are used to give extra help. They should be arranged so that they cut as many sections at as near right angles as possible. Those shown in Figs 22 and 23 are set at 45 deg to the vertical centreline but there is nothing special about that angle – it simply happened to suit here. Diagonals need not be parallel to each other, though they often are set out that way. Their endings at bow and stern are shown in Fig 23 as is the way they are measured – down their slope from the vertical centreline. Those measurements are generally set out on the plan view. As always, ensure that a nice, fair curve can be drawn through the spots. Define the slope and positioning of the diagonals in the sectional view on the lines plan.

Curve of areas

As a further check on the fairness of the hull a curve of areas may be drawn. The immersed areas at the various stations, as used in the displacement calculations, are set out from the centreline to any desired scale (see Fig 12). Thus, for instance, an area of 3 sq ft could be plotted at 3 in from the centreline using a scale of 1 sq ft = 1 in. When this has been done a curve is drawn through all the points.

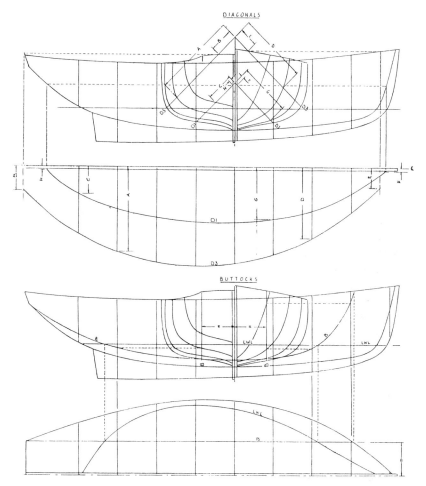

Fig 23   Details of how buttocks and diagonals are drawn
on a lines plan.

If a fair curve cannot be drawn, check first for mistakes
in the plotting or initial area calculation. If all is well in
those departments, it may be necessary to re-draw the lines
in the vicinity of the error in order to achieve a fair curve.

Drawing the lines

The freehand lines plan sketches, already done, will serve as a guide in the initial stages. The deck and rabbet in profile and plan and the load waterline in plan can be transferred in HB pencil from the sketch to this bigger scale drawing. A spline and possibly a curve or two will be needed for the operation.

Next draw in, freehand, what appeals as sectional shapes at, say, stations 1, 4 and 7 using the deck lines, rabbet and lwl as reference points. Now draw in Diagonal 2 (D2) and Buttock 1(B1) with a spline and perhaps a curve. Drawing sections at 1, 4 and 7 will have given clues as to where buttocks and diagonals should be fixed to get the best use out of them.

If the buttock and diagonal which you have just drawn fit the spots, and give a nice curve at the same time, you are on your way. Otherwise adjust the sections and other lines until everything agrees and looks pleasing.

Continue activities by turning your attention to, perhaps, D1 and AWL, which in this case is 6 in (152 mm) below LWL, and then to Buttock 2. There are still only three half-sections drawn but when the work so far suggested has been completed draw in the remaining sections and then D3 and the remaining waterlines, checking and correcting as you go.

If the half-sections are put in over the profile view, as shown, it will ease the task of checking that buttock height in section and profile agree and, if everything is drawn with a sharp HB pencil, rubbing out, and there will be plenty of that, won't be much of a problem.

Before going too far but when the sections look as if they are not likely to alter much more, check that the displacement is about what is wanted. Here a quick sortie into a displacement calculation, Table 9, gives a figure of just over a ton, which is roughly what is required. It is always better to have a boat potentially floating light rather than the other way around.

Drawing a lines plan for a round bilge is a fairly time-consuming business as an alteration in one place tends to alter half-a-dozen other things as well. But stick at it and your patience will be rewarded.

Table 9 Displacement calculation for a round bilge fin keel day sailer

Common interval, 2 ft $1\frac{1}{2}$ in = 2.125 ft

Station	Area sq. ft	S.M.	Product	Lever	Product
0	—	1	—	4	—
1	0.34	4	1.36	3	4.08
2	1.00	2	2.00	2	4.00
3	1.95	4	7.80	1	7.80
4	2.43	2	4.86	—	15.88 *Total*
5	2.28	4	9.12	1	9.12
6	1.44	2	2.88	2	5.76
7	0.37	4	1.48	3	4.44
8	—	1	—	4	—
			29.50 *Total*		19.32 *Total*

Displacement in cu. ft = $2/3 \times 2.125 \times 29.50 = 41.79$
Displacement in lb = $41.79 \times 64 = 2674$ in salt water (1.19 tons)
Longitudinal centre of buoyancy (lcb) = $\frac{19.32 - 15.88}{29.5} \times 2.125 = 0.25$
That is, lcb is 0.25 ft aft of midships (station 4)

Finally clean up the plan as much as possible and ensure that where lines cross the stations the crossing point is clear. Then dimension the stem and stern profiles as necessary and put in measurements wherever you think the boatbuilder will need them.

There will be a considerable sense of satisfaction when the lines plan is finished, and traced, but on its own, though decorative, it is not much use. What the builder wants is an offset table giving dimensions that he can use for making building moulds or that allow him to re-draw the vessel full size on the mould loft floor.

Offset table

A typical offset table layout, and one applicable to this boat, is shown in Fig 24. It is all quite straightforward but it helps if one person can measure and read out the offsets from the original

Station	0	1	2	3	4	5	6	7	8
				Half-breadths from ₵					
Deck at side						2-11-3			
LWL						2-10-2			
LWL						2-7-3			
Awl						2-0-1			
Rabbet						0-2-4			
				Heights above & below LWL					
Deck at side						1-3-6			
Buttock 1						⁻0-11-2			
Buttock 2						⁻0-6-1			
Rabbet						⁻1-5-3			
Bottom of keel						⁻3-6-4			
				Diagonals from ₵					
Diagonal 1						3-3-4			
Diagonal 2						2-4-0			
Diagonal 3						0-11-0			

Offsets in feet, inches and eighths to outside of planking. The suffix ⁻ in the heights table indicates the offset is below LWL.
Diagonals at 45 deg stations spaced at 2 ft $1\frac{1}{2}$ in.

Fig 24   How the offset table for the day sailer would be set out, with one column filled in.

lines plan (not the tracing) while someone else writes them down. Fig 25 shows the lines plans and Fig 26 the complete offset table for that 14 ft 6 in cruising dinghy of Chapter 2.

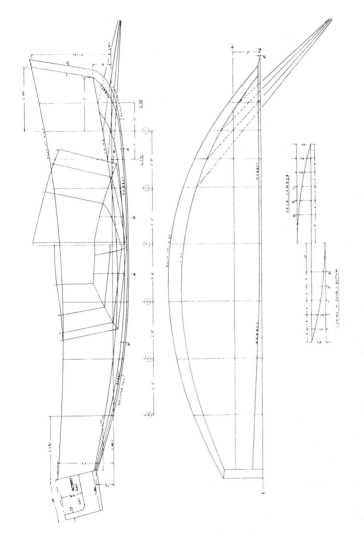

Fig 25 Lines plan of the cruising dinghy.

Two other lines plans for round bilge boats are shown in Figs 28 and 30. Fig 27 is a 19 ft (5.8 m) beach boat and Fig 28 its lines plan, in preliminary, rough form. Using the outlines of deck, keel, waterlines, buttocks and diagonal (and making sure

Station	½		1½						
Frame		1		2	3	4	5	6	7
Heights above & below LWL									
Deck at side	2-8-1	2-5-5	2-3-5	2-1-7	1-11-3	1-10-3	1-10-2	1-11-1	2-1-0
Chine	0-6-0	0-3-7	0-2-0	0-0-2	⁻0-2-0	⁻0-2-1	0-0-0	0-3-6	0-8-6
Buttock (B1)		0-0-4	⁻0-2-3	⁻0-3-6	—	—	—	—	—
Rabbet	⁻0-0-4	⁻0-3-3	⁻0-4-6	⁻0-5-6	⁻0-6-4	⁻0-6-3	⁻0-4-1	0-0-7	0-7-7
½ breadths from ℄									
Deck at side	1-1-7	1-10-3	2-5-1	2-10-2	3-4-2	3-5-1	3-1-6	2-6-3	1-5-4
Chine	0-9-2	1-5-2	1-11-5	2-4-4	2-10-1	2-11-3	2-8-4	2-2-1	1-4-7
Rabbet	0-1-0	0-1-0	0-1-0	0-1-0	0-1-0	0-1-2	0-2-2	0-3-3	0-4-4

Offsets in feet, inches and eighths to outside of skin in the heights table. The suffix ⁻ indicates the offset is below LWL.

Fig 26   Offsets for the 14 ft 6 in cruising dinghy.

the engine will go in where needed with a suitable propeller able to swing with adequate tip clearance, the proper lines plan is drawn. A final check on displacement is made and the offset table then drawn up.

We have concentrated almost exclusively so far on smallish boats. After all, the first-time designer is fairly unlikely to try his hand at a big and expensive world girdler or offshore race contender. But everything that has been said applies just as much to large as to small craft and Fig 29 shows a 66 ft (20 m) gaff schooner designed for work in the Arctic. Working sail area is about 2000 sq ft (185 m²). Fig 30 is her lines plan. She has a short counter stern as did the beach boat.

When the offset table is complete, draw the half-sections again to as large a scale as is convenient. Any inaccuracies will then become apparent and a study of the lines plan and, if necessary, some minor re-drawing should put things right. Remember to amend the offset table to take in these corrections.

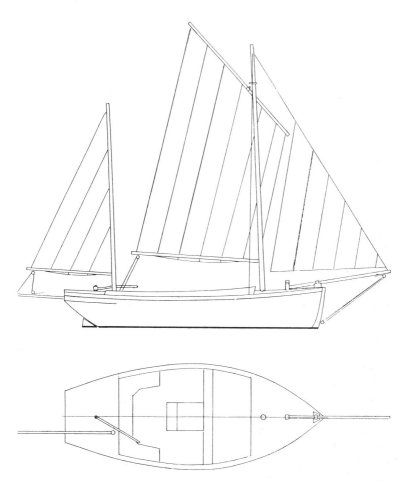

Fig 27   Profile of a 19 ft (5.8 m) beach boat.

On a chine boat, or one with frames rather than steamed timbers, it should help the builder if offsets are given at frames rather than at displacement stations. Though the latter will have to be drawn for displacement and LCB purposes they then would not be used for offsets. To be honest, a minority of builders actually loft the lines. They prefer to fair the vessel as they

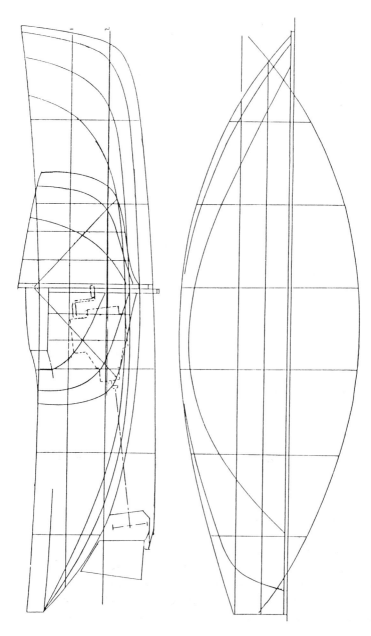

Fig 28   Preliminary lines plan of the beach boat.

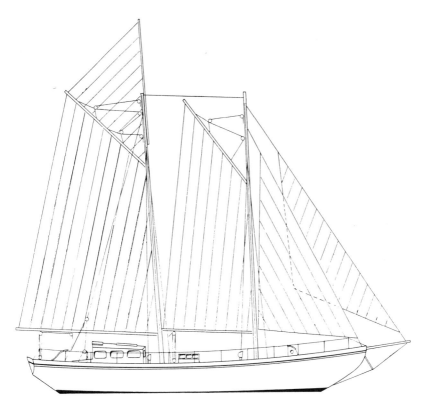

Fig 29   The gaff schooner for Arctic exploration.

build it and thus offsets to frames will save them time and save you money.

Hard chine lines plan

Fig 31 shows the centreboard version of the day sailer in chine form. Normally, but actually incorrectly, a vee bottom boat is shown as having straight line sections throughout. Thus only the deck, chine and rabbet lines are drawn, with straight lines defining the sections at each station. However, if a piece of card

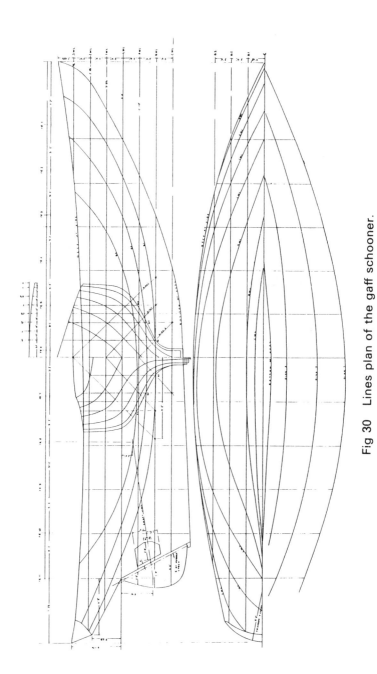

Fig 30 Lines plan of the gaff schooner.

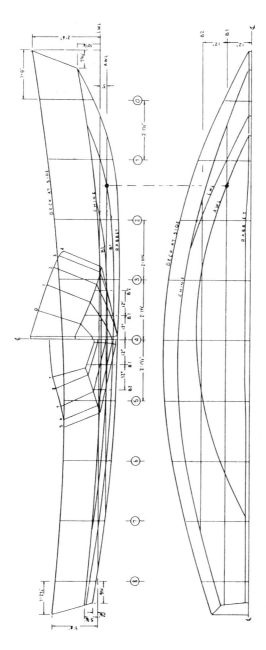

Fig 31 Hard chine version of the 20 ft day sailer with conically developed forward bottom.

is held so that the bottom edge represents the keel line and the top edge is then twisted into the shape of the chine at the bow, it will be seen that the card between the two is curved, meaning that in fact the sections between chine and keel are curved, not straight.

If this fact is ignored no waterlines, buttocks or diagonals need be drawn and the builder, flexing his muscles and employing a mighty army of cramps, will probably be able to distort the ply, or whatever it is, to conform to the straight frames. He may be forced into producing one or two with curved outer faces, using patterns made on the job.

On the other hand it is possible to predict the shape of the bottom frames together with the appropriate forefoot, having curves that the ply would be glad to follow.

Conic projection

This shape prediction is carried out using a conic projection (Fig 32) and what is derived from it is the correct form for the forward bottom. Elsewhere it is assumed that normal straight line sections will be satisfactory.

Draw in the chine line in plan and profile together with the rabbet in plan. The rabbet in profile can be lightly sketched in as a guide to the desired shape. Next we must find the apexes of the cone in plan and profile that will produce the hoped-for curve, especially round the forefoot. These apexes will always be below lwl, below the centreline in plan and to the right of station 0. Most importantly, the apexes must be in the same vertical line.

Spread a sheet of tracing paper over the lines plan and start experimenting. A generator from the apex in plan view to the intersection of chine line and station will cross the rabbet in plan at some spot. Project this point up to the same generator in profile and its intersection will give a point for the rabbet in profile. Generators are not normally drawn to further aft than midships and in Fig 26 the furthest they go is the chine on station 3.

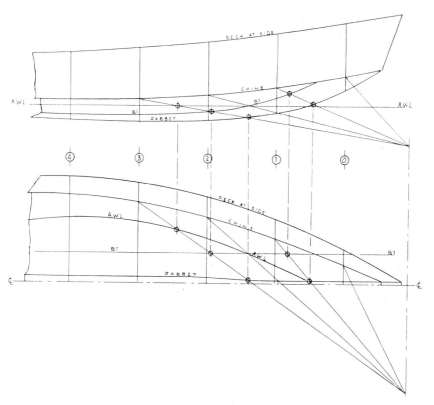

Fig 32   The apexes and generators of the cone.

You might find suitable apexes at the first or second attempt or only after a dozen or more. Move the apexes nearer or further from one another; away from or closer to station 0; and don't give up hope. Keep trying and what seemed ridiculous to begin with will suddenly work out.

When the curve of the forefoot seems satisfactory, attention should be turned to waterlines and buttocks. Their shape is determined by generator crossing points as with the rabbet. Have another look at Fig 32 and all should be revealed.

Only a length of forward bottom will have its shape governed by this conic projection scheme. From about midships aft the sections on this boat will be composed of straight lines because chine and rabbet are running reasonably parallel with little twist between them. On a double-ender though, another, handed, projection is usually needed aft. Fair any lengths where the sections are composed of straight lines into the curved areas in the normal manner. Fig 9 showed the apexes of the generators to form a conic projection for the forward bottom of the cruising dinghy. Work out the apex positions on the initial, small scale lines plan first or you may draw the larger scale lines on the paper such that the apexes of the cones are over the edge of the drawing board.

Centre of effort (CE) and 'lead'

The positioning of the sail plan should now be checked. It was previously stated that the mast should be a little forward of the toe of the keel or centreboard. That was fine but the time has come to place it more definitely than that.

Having first drawn the midships station line, cut out the underwater profile of the boat, including rudder, in tracing paper. Fold it a few times longitudinally, concertina fashion, and then balance it on a compass point. Prick this point through, unfold the paper, and that is the centre of lateral resistance (CLR) and the point about which the craft will pivot.

Then work out the area and centre of area of each sail. A gaff main can be divided into two triangles. The centre of area of a triangle is found by dividing a couple of sides into half and drawing lines to these midway points from their opposite corners (Fig 33). The intersection of the two lines marks the centre of area. Now measure the distance of each centre of area from a perpendicular through the forward ending of lwl and multiply that distance by the area of the sail. Add up those figures and divide the total by the total sail area.

This will give the position of the centre of effort (CE) from that forward perpendicular. Mark it on the underwater profile and measure the distance between CLR and CE. This distance divided by the waterline length, and then multiplied by 100,

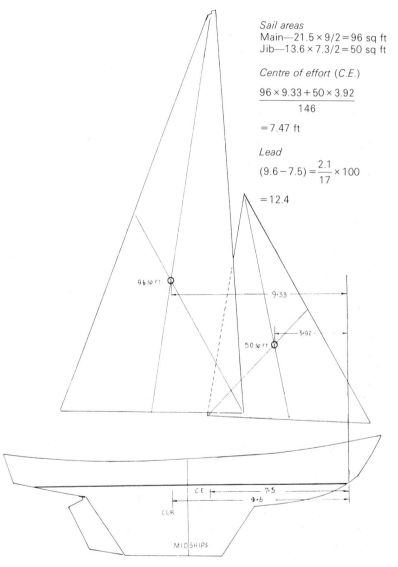

Sail areas
Main—21.5 × 9/2 = 96 sq ft
Jib—13.6 × 7.3/2 = 50 sq ft

Centre of effort (C.E.)

$$\frac{96 \times 9.33 + 50 \times 3.92}{146}$$

= 7.47 ft

Lead

$$(9.6 - 7.5) = \frac{2.1}{17} \times 100$$

= 12.4

Fig 33 Working out the position of the centre of effort (CE) and its lead over the centre of lateral resistance (CLR).

will give the percentage 'lead' of CE over CLR. The lead should be about 12–14 per cent for shallow hull, fin keel or centreboard craft; about 10 per cent for deeper more traditional yachts; and about 8 per cent for cruising yachts of classic form.

Finally in this section a couple of things that are occasionally useful to know. The first is tons per inch immersion (TPI). That is, the number of tons of added weight (or subtracted weight) which will cause the boat to sink or rise 1 inch in the water. It is assumed that the weight is placed on the longitudinal centre of buoyancy (lcb) and so does not cause a change in trim.

$$TPI = \frac{A}{420}$$

where A is the area of the waterplane at which the vessel is floating, in sq ft.

So if we had a craft 25 ft on the waterline with 8 ft waterline beam and the area of that waterplane was 140 sq ft:

$$TPI = \frac{140}{420}$$ which gives 0.33 tons or 746 lb.

Thus, if 746 lb were put on board or taken ashore the vessel would change draught by 1 in.

MCT predicts what shift in weight would produce a 1 inch change of trim.

$$MCT = 0.000175 \times \frac{A^2}{B}$$ approximately

where A is that waterplane area again and B is the waterline beam; in this case 140 sq ft and 8 ft respectively.

$$MCT = 0.000175 \times \frac{140^2}{8}$$ which works out at 0.43 tons ft.

Thus, if 0.2 tons were moved 6 ft that would be 0.2 × 6 tons ft, which is 1.2 tons feet and the change of trim would be 1.2/ 0.43, or 2.8 in, shared between bow and stern: bows up, stern down and vice versa pivoting about lcg.

4 Motor boat design

Chapters 1 to 3 have concentrated almost exclusively on sailing craft, so now we had better redress the balance and have a look at motor boats whilst reassuring those interested in power who have slogged through those opening chapters that their time has not been wasted. The mechanics of drawing lines plans, fairing them, and working out weights and displacement calculations are precisely the same, whatever type of boat is being designed. It is only the hull shape that may be different and even that is not always the case. The underwater form of a low speed motor boat will be similar to that of a sailing hull simply because with a limited amount of power available, whether from sails or engine, the hull has to offer as little resistance to moving through the water as possible.

Figs 34 and 35 show an example of the type. A river cruiser 27 ft 6 in by 10 ft 3 in (8.4 m × 3.1 m) with a displacement of 3 tons, she has a 10 hp motor to give a top speed of around $6\frac{1}{2}$ knots. Waterline length is 25 ft (7.6 m). The transom is just clear of the water and the buttocks are running up in gentle curves to clear the wash from around her stern with as little fuss as possible. Round bilge configuration would have been a slight advantage from the easy running point of view but she was built in aluminium alloy where using the material in sheet

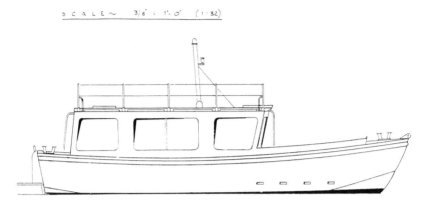

Fig 34   Above water profile of the 27 ft 6 in river cruiser.

form saves a fair amount of money; a consideration not to be sneezed at.

But when we grandly talk of low speed motor boats, what do we really mean? When does low speed become something else? Well, before answering that there is one term that must be understood.

Speed/length ratio

Here boat speed in knots (V) is compared with waterline length in feet (L). $V/\sqrt{L}$ is speed/length ratio. Thus a vessel 25 ft on the waterline at, say, 6 knots has a speed/length ratio of: $6/\sqrt{25}$ or 6/5 which is 1:2. At 10 knots her speed/length ratio is $10/\sqrt{25}$, giving an answer of 2. A 300 ft ferry at 20 knots has a speed/length ratio of: $20/\sqrt{300}$ which is 1:15, and so on.

This principally allows us to define the category of boat which will apply to a particular vessel, and so to design a hull that will

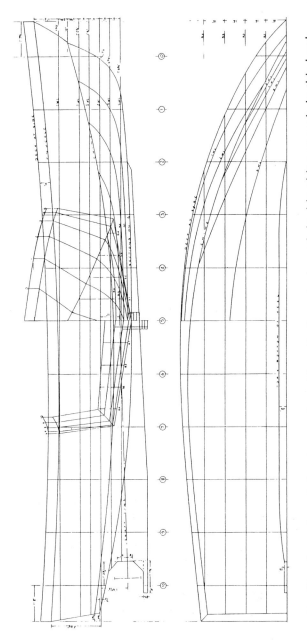

Fig 35 Lines plan of the river cruiser. Like all other single and double chine vessels in this book, the forward sections are conically developed.

suit this category. For this purpose we can define the categories as follows:

- *Low speed* – up to a speed/length ratio of about 1.6
- *Medium speed* – having a speed/length ratio of between 1.6 and 3
- *High speed* – with a speed/length ratio above 3

It will be appreciated that by using speed/length ratio all sorts of sizes and speeds can be neatly corralled together. A motor boat 30 ft on the waterline and doing 20 knots has a speed/length ratio of 3.6 and so can be classed as a high speed vessel but a 300-footer at the same 20 knots is running at a speed/length ratio of 1.15 and so is a low speed type, to be designed as such. For her to be considered high speed she would have to be doing:

$V/\sqrt{L} = 3$ (or more)

$V = 3 \times \sqrt{L}$ or $V = 3 \times 17.3$

$V = 52$ knots and even then would be comparatively slower than the 30-footer which was running at a speed/length ratio of 3.6.

Wave making

As a boat moves along it shoulders water aside and in doing so makes waves. One set of these pressure waves runs diagonally out from the bow and another, less noticeably, from the stern. A further, more important set, runs transversely along the vessel's sides with a crest visible at the bow followed by a trough and then another crest which may be, depending on the craft's speed, somewhere within the length of the hull or out past the stern. On a big boat especially, there may be several crests in the vessel's length initially but as speed rises the waves will lengthen until there is a crest at the bow and another at the stern and then only a single visible crest near the bow. The rest of the wave system will have passed astern. It takes power to

Table 10 Wave length depends on boat speed

Speed (knots)	Length (feet)	Speed (knots)	Length (feet)
6	20.0	12	80.1
7	27.2	14	109.6
8	35.6	16	142.4
9	45.0	20	222.5
10	55.6	25	347.7
11	67.3	30	500.6

make these waves and a heavy, bulky craft will make bigger and deeper waves than some light, lean counterpart.

The distance between wave crests, or the length of the waves, is governed entirely by boat speed, Table 10. So a 30 ft (9.1 m) boat at, say, 7 knots is creating a transverse wave system, the distance between whose crests (27.2 ft) is less than the length of the boat. At some speed between 7 and 8 knots the aft crest will have moved astern of the vessel and it will move further and further astern as speed rises. At, for instance, 10 knots the wave length between crests will be over 55 ft. The speed when the wave length is the same as the length of the hull is known as the vessel's displacement or hull speed. On a 40-footer it would be somewhere between 8 and 9 knots; on an 80-footer, 12 knots and so on. Specifically, the hull speed occurs at a speed/length ratio of 1.34. Any type of boat from dinghy to supertanker makes the same length of wave at the same speed. It is only the wave size that alters with vessel weight and form.

What happens in practice is shown in Fig 36. A boat about 21 ft (6.4 m) on the waterline is shown travelling first at about 6 knots. Table 10 indicates that at that speed the wave length is 20 ft and so the vessel is nicely supported by crests at bow and stern and will ride pretty well level. The lower sketch assumes speed has risen to 9 knots. Wave length is now 45 ft. The bow is still supported by the forward wave crest but the stern is in a hollow. The boat is trimming horribly bows-up and is essentially trying to travel uphill – a power-absorbing pursuit.

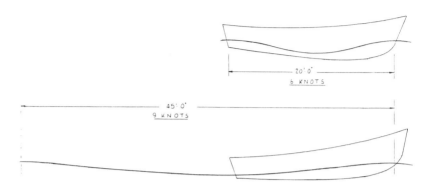

Fig 36   As boat speed increases the wave system becomes longer and the vessel trims by the stern.

Motor boat hulls

The usual, though not quite the only, way of overcoming this excessively bows-up attitude is to have a hull with a wide, buoyant transom and stern sections against which the oncoming water can exert a good upwards push. The boat will be presenting a wedge-shaped profile to this torrent with the result that it tends to lift the deepest part – the stern – and so reduces the high bow posture.

It can be imagined that the river cruiser of Figs 34 and 35 would present a sorry picture when attempting to reach velocities beyond those of her displacement speed. She would sit down with bows supported by the forward wave crest and general attitude such that her aft buttocks were lying flat on the wave slope.

Considerably better would be the small steel workboat of Fig 37. Though not designed for high speeds her run aft is reasonably flat and combined with an immersed transom she would travel at a steep but just about acceptable angle such that the oncoming water could act to lift her stern provided she had sufficient power installed.

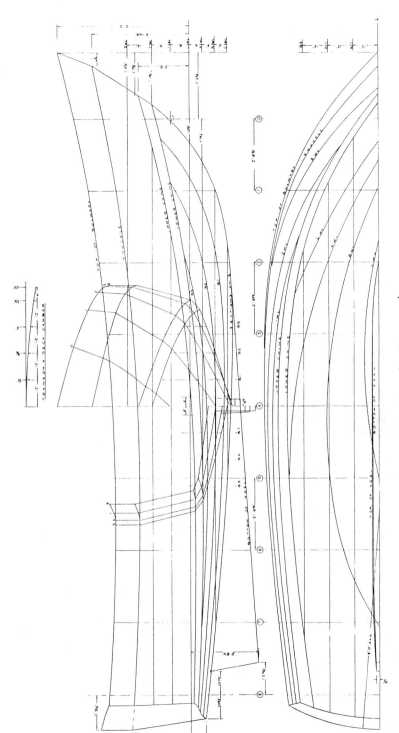

Fig 37 Lines plan of a 25 ft steel workboat capable of moderate speeds.

Better still in the pursuit of speed is a hull form where the aft buttocks run pretty well parallel to the designed waterline and the transom width is as great as anywhere in the boat, or nearly so. A slight taper towards the stern from the point of widest beam looks best but slight is the operative word. Fig 38 shows these features in a 27 ft ×9 ft (8.2 m ×2.7 m) speedboat hull designed for about 35 knots. Though not very apparent there is a small, flat area in the bottom aft, to promote early planing. Incidentally, a boat is said to be planing when the sides above the chine and the transom are running dry. Topsides forward should be given good flare to help promote a dry deck.

For good lift qualities curves both longitudinally and transversely are best avoided. Thus the buttock lines from somewhere near midships right back to the transom should be flat, too. A 'flattie' motor boat would be fine for messing about, or even dashing around at speed on calm waters and would plane very early but would be skittish in strong winds, there being virtually nothing of the boat in the water at high speeds. In rough water she would beat herself to pieces in no time at all. So practical boat hulls have to be given some vee or deadrise. The greater the vee the greater the loss of lift but the better the seakeeping qualities and, eventually, high deadrise angles can lead to improved high speed performance because they allow gradually reducing waterline beam. But more of that in the sections on beam and spray rails that follow.

To sum up, boats intended for medium speeds are designed with one eye on reasonable low speed qualities. That is, gradually rising buttocks aft and only quite lightly immersed transoms allow the water to clear the stern without too much power-sapping turbulence. Fast boats, on the other hand, are drawn with no consideration other than speed. Running lines aft are pretty well parallel to the designed waterline with a consequently deeply immersed transom. This drags a mess of water behind it at low speeds with dire effects on low speed performance.

A compromise form is shown in Figs 39 and 40. This is a medium speed cruiser – about 12 knots maximum which on a waterline length of 32 ft 6 in (9.9 m) gives a speed/length ratio

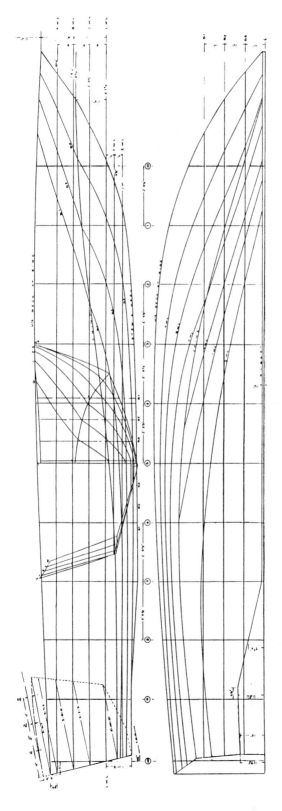

Fig 38   Lines plan of the 28 ft speedboat with single chine and designed for a speed of something like 35 knots.

Fig 39   A medium speed cruiser with 12 knots or so maximum.

of 2.1. Here the aft buttocks start by running upwards in the conventional manner but then straighten out to give a perfectly flat surface towards the transom. As the boat trims stern down in her climb up the speed range, this surface becomes angled down into the water stream and acts as a wedge to lift the stern. Such a system works fine after trials afloat to find the best size and angle for the wedge, which may subsequently be incorporated into the bottom shell or remain as separate (port and starboard) planted-on wedges. However, it can be imagined

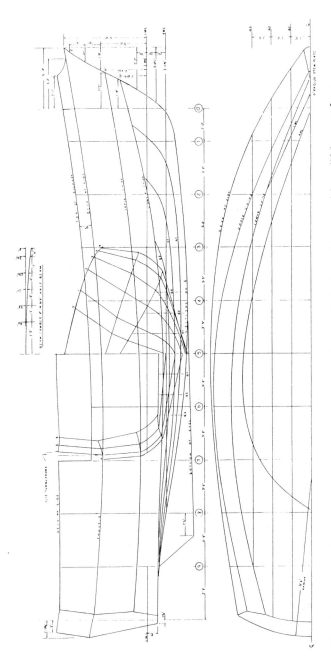

Fig 40   The medium speed cruiser with running lines aft flattened to provide a lifting surface which helps counteract excessive stern-down trim.

that wedges continue to perform until they are parallel with the waterline and thus no longer effective. If they had been angled down towards the stern to begin with they may cause the boat to trim down by the bow at speed, which would be dangerous and inefficient. A bows-up trim of between 2 and 4 degrees is usually the best all-round attitude.

In all cases a chine form is preferable and is vital for fast boats to keep the topsides above the chine running as dry as possible and thus lessening frictional resistance. A chine rail (Fig 41) materially assists. The greater the area of surface that is wetted by the sea, the more the power that is needed to drive the boat along. Where a double chine is used, as here on a medium speed vessel, to soften the abrupt change in shape that occurs with a single chine and so to lessen resistance, the rail runs above the upper chine. With round bilge form, a chine rail is absolutely necessary, running just above the turn of the bilge aft which should have as tight a radius as possible.

Many outdrives and bigger outboards incorporate some form of tilt mechanism where the angle of thrust from the propeller can be selected. Using such an arrangement alters the trim of

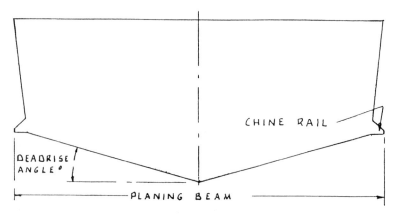

Fig 41   Definitions of some terms used when describing a motor boat's hull.

the boat and so helps in attaining the best running trim. Transom flaps can also be useful in controlling trim.

Low wave making types

At the beginning of this section we mentioned the length of the pressure wave caused by the boat's passage being governed solely by speed but its depth from crest to trough being related to its weight and form. If the wave depth was slight, the vessel would not have such a steep hill to climb. It thus follows that a lean and light craft would have fewer problems in achieving respectable speeds without bad trim problems on the way than a bluff heavyweight. This applies, of course, to motor craft as well as sailing vessels. With the latter, a conventional yacht, with outside ballast and power limited by the fact that it heels and loses power as the wind increases, can never overcome the trim problem. But something like a windsurfer, with a lightweight and svelte hull and with crew weight disposed such that it has the maximum effect on reducing heel, can very easily power through the pressure wave barrier. So too can, say, a lightweight catamaran where twin hulls resist undue heel and loss of power.

With motor boats it is very rare to see examples that take advantage of the possibility but, between World Wars I and II, Camper and Nicholsons built a range of sleek round bilge launches about 50 ft (15.2 m) in length with a narrow beam of about 8 ft (2.4 m). Constructed lightly in timber, these craft could manage 20 knots with a 100 hp engine; a very respectable speed/length ratio of 2.8 achieved by using a slim, low wavemaking hull.

As another example, using lightweight aluminium alloy construction, Universal Shipyards built some 26 ft (7.9 m) launches having a displacement of about 1.3 tons in the 50s and early 60s. With a 65 hp installed, these craft could manage 22 knots – a triumph for light displacement. This speed/length ratio of about 4.4 was achieved on a round bilge hull quite far removed from the ideal planing boat form, being simply bent up from what was essentially one sheet of alloy per side.

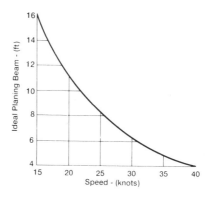

Fig 42 Ideal planing form beam for a 25 ft fast motor boat at various speeds.

Beam and lcb

Tank test work allows us to work out the ideal planing beam for any fast motor boat if we know its intended speed, displacement, deadrise, waterline length and position of the lcg. Fig 42 shows the result of a calculation for a vessel 25 ft (7.6 m) on the waterline with a displacement of four tons and with its lcg 55 per cent of the waterline length aft of the forward waterline ending; deadrise is 15 degrees.

So if 20 knots had been the designed operating speed, the average chine beam (Fig 42) between midships and the transom should be around 11 ft (3.3 m). If 30 knots had been the aim, a beam of just over 6 ft (1.8 m) would be more appropriate. All this probably usefully shows is that the usual overall length/overall beam ratio of 3:1 is about right for general use but that if really high operating speeds are anticipated reducing the beam is an advantage.

The lcb and lcg on virtually all motor boats should be about 55 per cent of the waterline length aft of the forward waterline ending.

Deadrise

This is the angle the bottom makes with the horizontal from its centreline ending (Fig 41 again) just as it is on sailing craft. In fact the angle is much the same, too, 15 degrees at midships being an average sort of figure, rising considerably at the bow and dropping slightly at the stern.

On fast boats the deadrise is often increased quite a lot in the interests of soft riding in rough water. It would be classed as a deep vee if that rise of floor were 22 degrees or more at midships. In such a case, deadrise at the transom would rarely be less than 18 degrees or so, while at the bow it would certainly be more but the chine would not lift as much as it does on lower midships deadrise boats.

Spray rails

On these deep vees, an interesting phenomenon occurs at speed. All fast boats lift bodily in the water above speed/length ratios of 3, or thereabouts, as the dynamic lift given by the water rushing past the bottom really takes hold. Most high speed craft sport spray rails running along the bottom to give a certain amount of lift and to deflect spray away from areas of the bottom that might otherwise be wetted. With steeply vee'd sections the time comes as speeds rise and the boat lifts in consequence that one set of spray rails deflects water so completely that the area of bottom above them runs dry. This, in effect, defines a new and narrower waterline beam which, as was mentioned in the previous section, is desirable at high speeds.

Eventually, of course, the next, lower set of spray rails may take over to create an even narrower beam and so on. This does not normally happen on craft with more modest deadrise angles because the water deflected by the rails simply forms again on the hull above the rails (Fig 43).

Spray rails are normally of triangular form with their bottom faces horizontal. They start at the chine in the form of

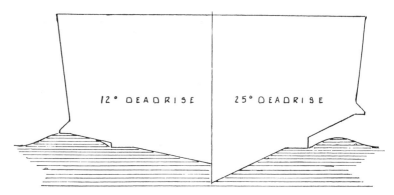

Fig 43 A spray rail can make water break away from the bottom of a deep vee hull but generally not on craft with shallower vees.

chine rails and are then set in pairs running, on modestly vee'd boats, from just aft of midships to as near the bow as can be managed without their fitting becoming too difficult. On deep vees they run full length, though near the keel where they stand no chance of defining a new beam they can be shortened in the interests of reducing wetted surface.

There is no need for these rails on low and medium speed craft where they can achieve very little of practical value but simply increase wetted surface.

Speed prediction

Table 11 gives bhp (brake horsepower) figures based on the waterline length and displacement of the craft. Thus, for instance, a motor boat 20 ft (6.1 m) on the waterline and displacing 1.5 tons would require 24 bhp to do 9 knots, provided she had a 'transom and flat stern' form. Translated into the categories we devised, these type headings would be, first, low speed form (canoe stern), then medium speed form and, finally, high speed form. The answers will be wrong if the hull shape is not of the

Table 11 The required brake horsepower needed for various speeds can be determined when waterline length and displacement are known

Length	Tons	Canoe stern		Transom and flat stern				Transom and very flat stern or chine form				V-chine or stepped	
		5	6	7	8	9	10	11	12	13	14	15	16	17
	0.5	1.0	1.7	2.9	4.7	7.2	10	12	14	17	19	22		
	1.0	1.8	3.6	6.6	10.8	16	20	24	28	33	39	44		
20 ft	1.5	2.6	5.7	11	17	24	30	36	43	50	58	67		
	2.0	3.1	8.0	15	22	32	40	48	57	67	77	89		
	3.0	3.7	12	24	33	48	59	72	85	100	116	134		
	2.0	2.4	5.0	10	17	25	34	42	50	59	68	78		
25 ft	3.0	3.0	6.5	15	26	37	48	61	74	88	102	115		
	4.0	4.0	8.7	22	36	50	64	84	100	117	136	155		
	5.0	5.0	12	28	46	65	85	105	125	146	170	196		
	1.5	1.6	2.9	4.9	7.4	11	15	23	31	37	43	50	57	
	2.0	1.9	3.6	6.4	10.4	15	22	32	42	50	58	67	76	
	3.0	2.5	5.0	9.7	17	26	36	48	62	75	87	100	114	
30 ft	4.0	3.0	6.4	13	26	37	51	64	83	100	116	133	152	
	5.0	3.3	7.7	16	32	46	66	80	104	125	145	167	190	
	6.0	3.5	8.8	19	39	56	79	96	125	150	174	200	227	
	8.0	4.0	11	26	51	74	105	128	166	200	232	267	303	
	4.0	2.8	5.2	8.5	13	20	28	39	53	67	84	97	110	124
	6.0	3.5	7.0	12	20	34	50	55	89	105	126	144	164	186
	8.0	4.0	8.4	15	26	47	73	94	119	145	168	193	219	248
	10.0	4.4	9.9	18	33	61	92	122	149	180	210	242	274	310
40 ft	12.0	4.6	11	21	40	75	110	146	179	217	252	290	329	372
	14.0	5.0	12	24	46	87	128	170	208	252	294	338	384	434
	16.0	5.2	13	27	53	100	147	195	238	289	336	387	439	465
	18.0	5.6	14	30	59	112	165	219	268	325	378	435	494	558
	20.0	5.9	15	33	66	125	183	244	298	361	420	484	548	620
	8.0	4.1	7.2	13	19	28	39	55	74	99	124	150	177	205
	10.0	4.6	7.9	15	23	35	53	76	100	130	162	193	228	257
	12.0	5.0	8.8	17	27	42	66	96	122	164	199	243	283	309
	14.0	5.3	9.6	20	30	49	82	116	155	198	243	286	330	360
	16.0	5.6	10	21	34	56	98	137	183	234	278	327	376	412
50 ft	18.0	5.8	11	23	38	63	112	168	212	270	313	368	423	463
	20.0	6.0	12	25	41	70	128	192	248	300	348	408	470	515
	25.0	6.5	13	30	50	87	164	240	312	375	435	510	588	643
	30.0	7.0	14	34	57	105	197	288	374	450	522	612	705	775
	35.0	8.0	15	37	66	123	230	336	437	525	609	715	823	900

Speed in knots

type specified. These are calm water power requirements and can probably be doubled for practical purposes.

The table can also be used as a guide to auxiliary power on yachts with some caution. A yacht may have considerably more windage than a motor boat due to her masts and rigging (though that wouldn't be so with those motor boats where box is piled upon box in the way of coachroofs, flying bridges, radar masts and so forth) and will almost certainly have greater wetted surface with her ballast keel.

For speeds higher than those covered by Table 11 a formula can be used. This is:

$$V = 124.7 \times \frac{P^{0.551}}{W^{0.476}}$$

where V is boat speed in mph; W is displacement in pounds; and P is shaft horsepower (about 10 per cent less than brake horsepower).

As an example let's take a boat with a displacement of 2000 lb with 150 shp installed. The sum then works out as:

$$V = 124.7 \times \frac{150^{0.551}}{2000^{0.476}}$$

That is: $V = 124.7 \times 15.8/37.3$. $V = 52.8$ mph or $52.8 \times 5280/6080 = 45.9$ knots, there being 5280 ft in a statute mile and 6080 ft in a nautical mile.

The formula can be turned round to find power, given a displacement and required speed. Thus:

$$P = \sqrt[0.551]{\frac{W^{0.476} \times V}{124.7}}$$

Put in the speed required (V, in mph) and you have your answer.

There is another way of predicting speed on a fast motor boat – actually, there are many alternative methods, but this is an easy one and gives good enough answers for first approximations on a new design. Predictions for a stepped hull form are also indicated for interest and to demonstrate that the conventional hard chine bottom is not the only

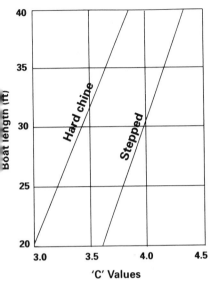

Fig. 43a   Speed prediction
curves for fast motor boats are
based on C values: length,
displacement and bhp. It is
assumed that the hull form is
suited to the planned speed
and that the boats are running
at speed/length ratios of 3.0 or
over. Speed/length ratio is
$V/\sqrt{L}$ and was discussed at
the beginning of the chapter
on motor boat design. The
method of using the 'C' values
obtained in this graph is
explained on page 86.

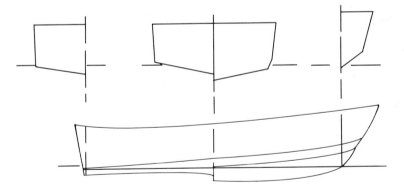

Fig. 43b   A double chine stepped hull. The step should carry
about 90 per cent of the vessel's weight with the remainder
being carried by the transom. This sounds complicated but in
practice means only that fixed weights such as engines,
batteries and so on are distributed such that they are
concentrated mainly in the step area.

shape for high speeds. There will be a little more on stepped forms shortly.

As an example of how the sums are done, assume that the power to drive a vessel with a 30 ft (9.1 m) waterline and $3\frac{1}{2}$ ton displacement at 30 knots is required. Bhp is brake horsepower.

$$\text{bhp} = \text{Displacement} \times \frac{V^2}{C^2} \text{ or}$$

$$\text{bhp} = 3.5 \times \frac{30^2}{3.4^2} \text{ which is 272 bhp.}$$

The 'C' value for 30 ft boat length is about 3.4 as shown on the diagram.

If power is known and likely speed wanted the method becomes, on a 25-footer (7.6 m) displacing 2 tons and with 250 bhp installed:

$$V = C \times \sqrt{\frac{\text{bhp}}{\text{displacement}}} \text{ or}$$

$$V = 3.25 \times \sqrt{\frac{250}{2}} \text{ which gives 36 knots.}$$

Stepped hulls

From the diagram used to predict speed it looks as if stepped hulls are inately faster than conventional forms, which is true. Fig 43b shows what a stepped hull looks like. It has a transverse step in the bottom roughly at 'midships and 3 in to 4 in deep (75–100 mm). Water rushing back along the bottom at high speeds drives off the step, re-forming again on the bottom some way aft of the step. Between these two areas the bottom should be running dry with a subsequent drop in wetted surface and increased speed potential.

The unwetted bottom area needs to be well ventilated through natural vents and even, perhaps, engine exhausts or a semi-vacuum may be set up behind the step when a wave momentarily blanks off both sides. This type is not very happy at low velocities when there will be turbulence behind the step but as a speedy hull form it has been unjustly neglected and deserves to be explored again.

In the First World War the MTB's of the day were the Thornycroft-built 40 ft (12.2 m) CMB's (Coastal Motor Boats) which on a displacement of nearly 4 tons and with engine power totalling 250 bhp were capable of 34 knots.

Propellers

The best people to advise on propellers are the manufacturers. This advice, based on experience as well as calculation, will be free if you order from them but it is often useful to have a good idea of the likely diameter from early on in the design process. The aperture for the prop can then be drawn with confidence. Tip clearance between hull and propeller blade should be at least 20 per cent of the diameter. So a 20 in diameter propeller would need a gap of 4 in between blade tips and hull.

A useful guide is as follows: a propeller should turn at between 80 and 100 rpm for every mph of boat speed. Hence a craft designed for 8 mph (6.9 knots) would be happy and efficient with a prop turning at somewhere around 800 rpm. This implies a large diameter, as will be seen, which would seriously hamper progress on a sailing boat with auxiliary engine but would be proper on a motor launch. There is no requirement to stick closely to any answer provided by that guide but it is worth keeping at the back of your mind. In general it is more efficient to accelerate a large column of water slowly than a small column fast.

Table 12 gives a guide to likely prop diameters based on propeller rpm and brake horsepower. For example, let us suppose we have a 20 bhp engine which develops this power at 2500 rpm. Possible reduction gears are 1.5:1, 2:1 and 3:1. What would be suitable propeller diameters?

Table 12 Suitable propeller diameters for various powers of engine coupled with propeller rpm

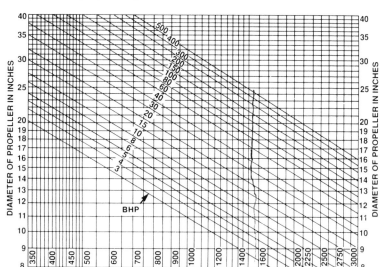

With 1.5 : 1 reduction the prop will be turning at 1666 rpm. At 20 hp that gives about 13 in as a suitable diameter. Assuming 2 : 1, the prop would be turning at 1250 rpm and the diameter would be around 15 in and with 3 : 1 reduction and 833 rpm, 19 in diameter might fill the bill. And so on.

The choice of associated propeller pitch, which is governed by slip, prop rpm and boat speed is best left to the experts (ie the manufacturers).

Tunnel sterns

In the case of very shoal-draught motor boats, it may be impossible to swing a decent propeller under the hull. There are two possible solutions. The first is to sweep the bottom up, rather as in Fig 40 and tuck the propeller under the high point of the

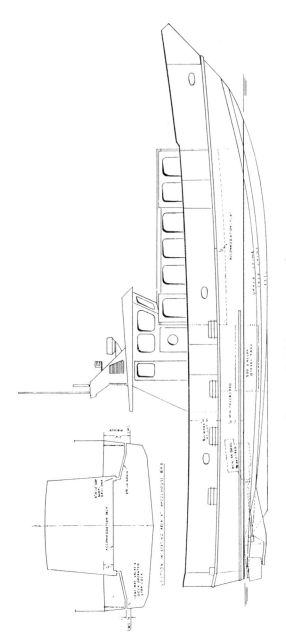

Fig 44   A 60 ft passenger ferry.

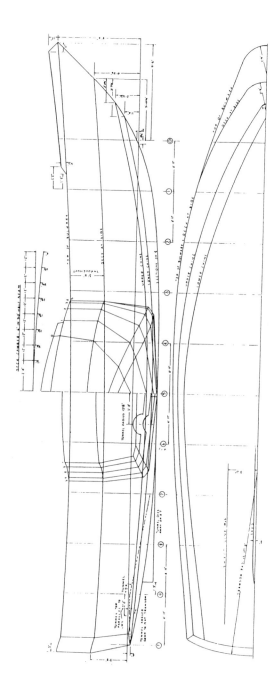

Fig 45   Lines plan of ferry with tunnel stern.

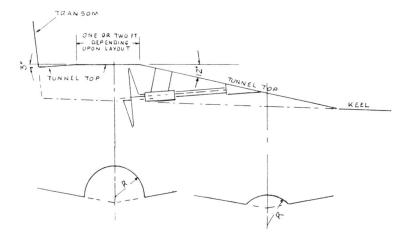

Fig 46 The basic form of a tunnel stern.

hull. The disadvantage of this is that it loses a lot of buoyancy aft, which may push the lcb rather far forward.

The alternative is to employ a tunnel stern. Here a normal hull shape is drawn and the propeller(s) housed in partial tunnels set into the bottom. Figs 44 and 45 show this in practice on a 60 ft × 18 ft (18.3 m × 5.5 m) ferry where loaded draught was restricted to 2 ft 6 in (0.8 m). As can be seen, this was a twin-screw vessel. Fig 46 gives the basic shape of a typical tunnel which can be planted in almost any hull. The propeller, incidentally, should be a snug fit in the tunnel with blade tip clearance of not more than about 1 in (25 mm). The top of the tunnel may be as high as the load waterline or even slightly above it but its exit should be submerged or the propeller may suck in air as well as water when going astern, with obvious effects on performance.

5 Resistance, sail plans and hull balance

In Chapter 4 we looked at the habit boats have of producing power-sapping waves as they move through the water. That chapter dwelt mainly on speeds above displacement speeds which, to jog your memory, is when a boat is travelling at a speed/length ratio of 1.34. But wave-making occurs at all speeds and its resistance to motion is termed wave-making or residuary resistance. The other component of total resistance is frictional resistance and is caused by the friction between water and hull, plus all its appendages such as rudders, keels, centreboards, propellers, shafts and so forth.

Resistance

What follows may seem rather high-flown but it does have practical implications, which will be revealed in the following sections.

Fig 47 shows resistance curves for a typical motor boat. Curves for a centreboard sailing vessel would be of similar form

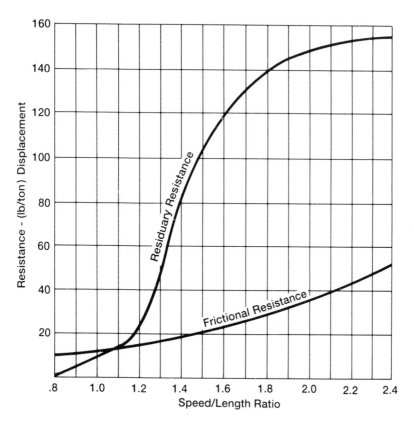

Fig 47 Resistance curves for a boat travelling at speed/length ratios of up to 2.4. This covers most sailing types and some powered vessels, particularly commercial craft.

but a deep-keel yacht would have a greater frictional component. It will be seen that the proportion of total resistance contributed by frictional and residuary (wave-making) resistance depends on speed/length ratio. Initially, frictional resistance is the greater absorber of power but at a speed/length ratio of about 1.05 their effects are about equal and above that ratio wave-making becomes the predominant feature. Resistance is given in lb per ton of displacement and can be converted to horsepower in the formula $BHP = 2 \times R \times V/550$, where R is resistance in pounds and V is the speed of the vessel in feet per second. Multiply knots by 1.68 to get ft/s. Thus 8 knots is 8×1.68, or 13.44 ft/s.

Looking at those curves total resistance at a speed/length ratio of 0.8 (4 knots on a 25-footer) is about 9 lb for friction and 2 lb for wave-making or residuary resistance. The grand total, then, is 11 pounds per ton and if the boat's displacement were 5 tons, total resistance would be $11 \times 5 = 55$ lb. Translated into brake horsepower that is:

$$BHP = \frac{2 \times 55 \times 4 \times 1.68}{550} = 1.34$$

'4×1.68' is converting 4 knots into ft/s.

At a speed/length ratio of 1.4 (roughly hull speed and representing 7 knots on our 25-footer), frictional resistance is 19 lb/ton and residuary, about 80 lb/ton. Totalling these numbers we get 99 lb/ton or $99 \times 5 = 495$ lb for a five-tonner. So:

$$BHP = \frac{2 \times 495 \times 7 \times 1.68}{550} = 21.2$$

Thus to achieve a modest 3 knots increase in speed, power requirements have gone up nearly 16 times. These are calm water figures, of course.

Length clearly plays a vital part in resistance and consequent power requirements. At the same speed/length ratio boats of similar form will have roughly equal resistance per ton of displacement. That is, a 25-footer at 5 knots, say; a 49-footer at 7 knots; and a boat 81 ft on the waterline at 9 knots would require the same horsepower per ton of displacement though speed has nearly doubled.

When thinking of how to get the best out of the size of boat being considered, there is not a lot that can be done in the design stage to reduce frictional resistance. The shape giving least wetted area for a given displacement is the arc of a circle but that is not a practical form for the sections except, perhaps, on multi-hulls where rolling and heeling are controlled by the existence of the two hulls. A chine may marginally assist a motor boat even at these low speed/length ratios and it is sensible to keep the length of exposed propeller shaft as short as possible, but really we'd do better concentrating on wave-making. Here we can influence the outcome quite considerably by drawing a hull where the fore and aft distribution of displacement best suits the likely speed/length ratio. This is done by seeking guidance from what is known as the prismatic coefficient.

Prismatic coefficient

This is the ratio of the immersed volume to the area of the midship section multiplied by waterline length. A fine C_p (prismatic coefficient) indicates a full midship section, implying that the displacement is concentrated around midships. A full C_p, on the other hand, suggests a fine midships section and full ends. This is the formula:

$$C_p = \frac{\text{Disp.} \times 35}{L \times A_m}$$

where displacement is in tons which the multiplier, 35, converts into cubic feet; L is waterline length, in feet; and A_m is the area of the midships section below the waterline, in square feet. As with all such formulae, the imperial measurements can be replaced by metric units to give the same answer.

Just as an example we could work out the sum for that 60 ft passenger ferry of Figs 44 and 45. Displacement there was 32 tons, waterline length 49.2 ft and area of midships section 37.2 sq ft. So putting those numbers into the formula:

$$C_p = \frac{32 \times 35}{49.2 \times 37.2}$$

$$C_p = 0.61$$

Design service speed was around 10 knots, giving a speed/length ratio of 1.4.

Fig 48 shows the ideal prismatic coefficient at various speed/length ratios and it will be seen that for the ferry and a ratio of 1.4, the C_p would ideally be 0.63, so that considering the many practical restraints inherent in a shoal draught commercial vessel our 0.61 isn't too far out.

That aiming for the best prismatic coefficient is not just an exercise in one-upmanship is shown by trials carried out on four 65 ft (19.8 m) fishing boats, Table 13. All except the Admiralty boat had a displacement of about 71 tons and with a waterline length of 62 ft and speed of 9 knots, speed/length ratio was 1.14. Glancing at Fig 48, it appears that the ideal C_p for such a ratio would be about 0.54 and that indeed was what *Silver Searcher* had. This enabled her to reach 9 knots with only 75 bhp. The others needed over 100 bhp for the same speed and in two cases considerably over.

You might also have noticed that the low prismatic of *Silver Searcher* has led to her having a half-angle of entrance at the waterline of 9 degrees compared with the other's angle of over 20 degrees. This angle is the one the load waterline makes with the centreline at its forward ending; half angle because the

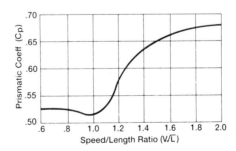

Fig 48   Optimum prismatic coefficients at different speed/length ratios.

Table 13 Details of four similar fishing boats evaluated against each other. From the standpoint of hull efficiency *Silver Searcher* was the clear winner with her low prismatic coefficient and small half angle of entrance

Feature	Admiralty type 65 ft MFV	Original G L Watson design	Modified G L Watson design Silver Scout	Herring board design Silver Searcher
Length overall	64 ft 6 in	65 ft 0 in	65 ft 0 in	65 ft 0 in
Length waterline	60 ft 0 in	62 ft 0 in	62 ft 0 in	62 ft 0 in
Maximum beam	17 ft 10 in	17 ft 10 in	17 ft 10 in	17 ft 10 in
Draught forward	4 ft 3 in	4 ft 9 in	4 ft 9 in	5 ft $8\frac{1}{2}$ in
Draught aft	7 ft 0 in	7 ft 3 in	7 ft 3 in	7 ft $2\frac{1}{2}$ in
Displacement	50 tons	71 tons	71 tons	71.5 tons
Block coefficient	0.35	0.383	0.378	0.359
Prismatic coeff.	0.62	0.645	0.612	0.537
Midship coeff.	0.56	0.594	0.617	0.675
Bhp for 9 knots	120	123	105	75
$\frac{1}{2}$ angle of entrance at w/line	23 deg	26 deg	21 deg	9 deg

angle is measured on one side only. Table 14 gives the desirable half angle of entrance at various speed/length ratios.

Prismatic coefficient is just as important on sailing craft as on powered vessels. A cruising yacht is reckoned to travel at a speed/length ratio of 1.0 to 1.15 as an average while a more racing orientated vessel might increase these ratios to 1.25 or 1.35. Such figures would suggest prismatics of about 0.53 to 0.55 and 0.58 to 0.63 respectively. A happy compromise would be a prismatic of 0.58. This would be fine if all yachts had canoe bodies and standard fin keels, but keels may be long or short, fat or thin, deep or shallow or any combination. This has an unsettling effect on the formula. Help is at hand, though, for an American naval architect, J E Paris, from a study of many successful designs, developed a curve showing the best relationship between prismatic coefficient and what is called lateral plane coefficient.

Table 14 Desirable half angles of entrance at various speed/length ratios

Speed/length ratio	Half angle of entrance (deg)
0.5	30
0.6	26
0.7	22
0.8	18
0.9	14
1.0 to 2.0	10

This coefficient is the ratio of the lateral plane in profile (including the rudder, other than remotely hung spade rudders, but excluding centreboards) and the circumscribing rectangle. The latter is waterline length multiplied by maximum draught.

Going back to that 20 ft day sailer (Fig 22) the lateral plane area is 33 sq ft; the waterline length, 17 ft; and maximum draught, 3.5 ft. Work that out; C_{1p} is lateral plane coefficient.

$$C_{1p} = \frac{33}{17 \times 3.5}$$

$$C_{1p} = 0.55$$

An approximation of the Paris curve is given in Fig 49 and so what is needed now is the prismatic coefficient for that 20-footer.

That is worked out easily enough. Displacement is 1.19 tons; waterline length 17 ft; and midship section underwater area, 4.86 sq ft.

$$C_p = \frac{1.19 \times 35}{17 \times 4.86}$$

$$C_p = 0.5$$

The midships section area can, of course, be taken direct from the displacement calculation corrected for scale, if necessary, and doubled because only half areas were used then.

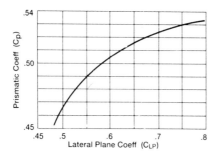

Fig 49 Desirable prismatic coefficients plotted against lateral plane coefficients.

Back to the Paris curve for prismatic and lateral plane coefficient, which shows that for a C_{1p} of 0.55 the optimum C_p would be about 0.49. Since ours was 0.5 that can be considered satisfactory.

Just before embarking on one more consideration of hull form, that of balance when heeled, it might be a relief to have a brief and possibly contentious look at the rig of yachts.

The rig

No apologies are offered for the fact that the various sail plans given throughout this book are all, by today's standards, a bit odd. Gaffs, lugs, sliding gunters . . . and not a single example of the omnipresent Bermudian or triangular main set-up. For those, all one has to do is to look round the nearest marina. There they are in their hundreds, with their associated hi-tech masts and rigging. Yet is this concentration on a single type really justified?

For going to windward, high aspect-ratio rigs are efficient and, within reason, the higher the ratio the better. Aspect-ratio

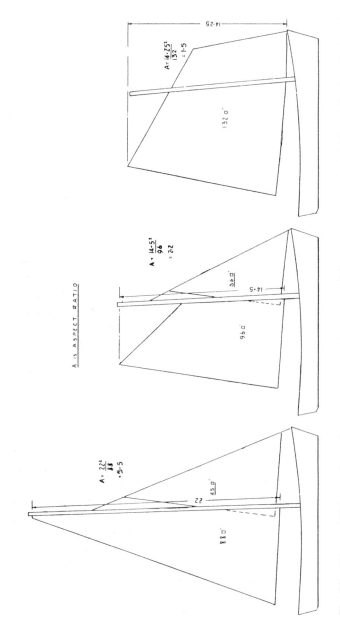

Fig 50   Three different rigs of the same area but very different aspect-ratios. The right-hand sketch shows a dipping lug.

is the length of the luff of the sail squared and then divided by the sail area; Fig 50 shows the aspect-ratio on various rigs. But sailing trials on full-size craft and wind tunnel tests seem to show that while a high aspect-ratio is beneficial when the craft is driving to windward with hardened sheets, as the vessel heads off and sheets are eased it becomes steadily less important. With the boom off at about 35 degrees to the centreline an aspect-ratio as low as 1 is quite acceptable. This is the sort of figure that might be achieved with gaff, sprit and lugsail rigs.

Should a rig be selected solely on the grounds of its better windward performance while disregarding its complexity, cost and, dare one say, uninspiring looks? Be that as it may, there are craft on which high aspect-ratio rigs are nearly always justified and these are the speedsters of this world: racing multi-hulls, some lightweight dinghies, ice yachts, land yachts and anything else at all with pretensions to real flashing speed. These craft pull the wind ahead and increase its apparent strength on many headings so that they are, to all intents and purposes, going to windward when their more sedate brethren are still ambling along on uneventful reaches.

Fig 51 shows this in diagrammatic form. It is assumed that a vessel is sailing along in an 18 knot breeze blowing from just forward of the beam. If she was making 6 knots the apparent wind would be from slightly more ahead and would be blowing at what appeared to be 20.5 knots. If she could pick up her skirts still further and manage 15 knots in this breeze, the apparent wind would have drawn even further ahead at a speed of 26.5 knots. Increase velocity to 20 knots and the now 30.25 knot apparent wind will be coming from about 45 degrees off the bow. So some specialised craft can actually sail faster than the true wind speed and by bringing the breeze ahead spend a lot of their sailing life effectively going to windward. On these boats an aspect-ratio of up to 7 is appropriate. More generally a ratio of 5 to 5.5 on Bermudian rigs is a happy compromise between the conflicting demands of efficiency and reasonably priced rigs where masts can be simply stayed.

If the reader is designing a boat purely for his (or her) own enjoyment without a thought for commercial success where

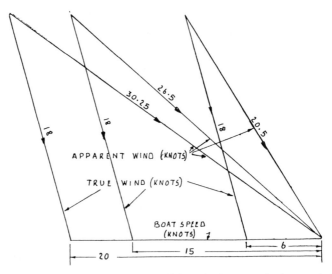

Fig 51   The faster a boat can sail in relation to wind speed the more she will bring the wind ahead.

custom and convention rule the day, do not be afraid to experiment with the rig. As long as the hull is of fairly normal form and the lead of the centre of effort over the centre of lateral resistance suggested in Chapter 3 is vaguely adhered to, even the oddest of rigs should produce some reasonable results. And there is one avenue still worth exploring. Twist in a sail where the top sags off to leeward compared with its well controlled bottom (set on a boom or similar), reduces its efficiency considerably. Such twist, though not generally too bad, is difficult to overcome on a Bermudian sail. On a gaff sail, though, twist is commonly much worse, which accounts in part for its inferior performance to windward, but is easier, theoretically, to control. A vang from the peak of the main gaff to the mizzen masthead might do the trick with an alternative of vangs port and starboard down to the yacht's quarters. If this twist could be eliminated entirely, gaff and lugsail rigs could well be more efficient than Bermudian, even to windward.

Having considered one aspect of hull form and prismatic coefficient, with a foray into sail plans, we might now shift our attention back to hulls and their reaction to the heeling forces applied by sails.

Hull balance

In Chapter 3, recommendations were made for the 'lead' of the centre of effort (CE) over the centre of lateral resistance (CLR). This put the CE a certain distance ahead of the CLR, which is correct in practice. But if the boat pivots about her CLR and the drive of the sails is through the CE, putting the CE ahead of the CLR should produce a most undesirable lee helm with the bow constantly falling off the wind (Fig 52) and only dousing the headsail, say, would allow the much preferable weather helm.

In practice, then, the CLR must shift forward of its assumed, theoretical position until it is ahead of the CE. This happens automatically on the vast majority of boats because of build-up of water pressure near the lee bow when driving along under sail. The phenomenon may be exaggerated on very bluff-bowed craft where the usual lead of CE over CLR can usefully be increased by way of compensation.

A boat is safer, comes about faster, and has superior windward ability with a small amount of weather helm (where the bow wants to come up into the wind). It is safer because in an emergency with the tiller or wheel abandoned the yacht will swing up into the wind and stop. She will come about faster because her natural inclination is to start the manoeuvre which only has to be completed with crew participation; and her better performance can be explained as follows. Assume that the weather side is to starboard. Weather helm means that the rudder blade is over to port, as in Fig 52, keeping the boat on a straight course and dissuading the bow from swinging into the wind. Water pressure on the inclined blade will create a sideways drift to starboard which resists leeway.

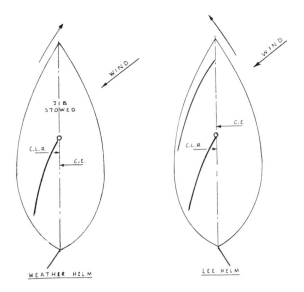

Fig 52   In practice, despite the contrary positioning when planning a sail layout, the centre of effort (CE) must lie aft of the CLR or lee helm would result.

As a yacht heels, she normally puts quite buoyant stern quarters into the water which are ill-matched by the comparatively lean bow. The result is that the vessel trims down by the head and surges up into the wind. On some craft, with exaggerated differences in form between bow and stern, the resulting bows-down attitude is fairly drastic with almost uncontrollable weather helm. The rudder may even be raised so high by this action that it becomes more or less useless in controlling the situation. This is obviously not to be recommended and the likelihood of its happening can be estimated by carrying out what is called a Rayner analysis.

On the sections of the craft are drawn heeled waterlines inclined at, perhaps, 15 degrees as in Fig 53. Here it has been done for both the round bilge and hard chine versions of the 20 ft day sailer (Figs 22 and 33). The areas of the immersed

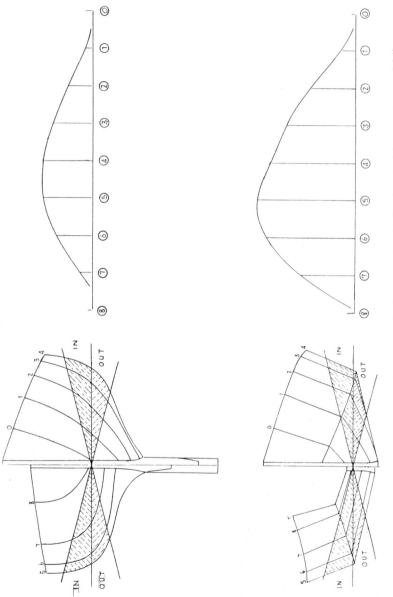

Fig 53 A Rayner analysis for hull balance carried out on both the hard chine and round bilge versions of the 20 ft day sailer.

('in') and emerged ('out') wedges are measured for each section. The figures for station 5 are, just as an example, 1.93 sq ft and 0.825 sq ft, respectively, on the chine version and 1.74 sq ft ('in') and 1.22 sq ft ('out') for the round bilge type. The areas of the 'out' wedges are then subtracted from those of the 'in' wedges and those answers plotted at some suitable scale out from a base line. Thus on the chine boat the point on station 5 will be 1.93 − 0825 = 1.105 out from the base. And so on. A curve is drawn through all the points thus given and the result studied for excesses of area aft of the midships station. Most vessels will show some greater area aft and the greater this imbalance, the more uninhibited will be the surges up to windward.

It will be seen that in our examples, the round bilge double-ender shows little difference in those areas forward and aft of midships. Therefore the boat is likely to be well balanced and easy on the helm. The chine type, on the other hand, has a considerable excess of area aft and will probably have a fair amount of weather helm, especially when well heeled over. The excess of 'in' wedge area is concentrated around station 5, not far aft of midships. If it had been still further aft the tendency to drive up to windward would increase.

A glance at the two sets of sections will demonstrate what has to be done to bring the chine type nearer to the round bilge standard of balance, but do not labour too hard to achieve what, on paper, might appear to be a perfectly balanced hull. Some weather helm is desirable while, occasionally, factors come into play affecting balance which do not show up in drawing or calculation. Practically, in the last resort with a hideously unbalanced hull, vastly increasing the size of the rudder may prove a solution. Not only does this give the helmsman greater leverage to control the boat's antics but it brings the CLR further aft which is generally desirable in such cases.

Aspect-ratio of hull appendages

Especially for windward work 'lift' from keel, centreboard and even the rudder are important factors for good performance and the more lift the better. So for this element of sailing it is worth taking advantage of the fact that area for area these hull appendages are most efficient if they have a high aspect-ratio, which in this case is depth^2/area.

The limiting factor is practicality. Though it would be nice to have a centreboard, say, with an aspect-ratio of 6, such a structure is rather prone to damage. On a craft intended for deep water operation damage may be unlikely and a high aspect board drawn with a clear conscience.

Fins, rudders, centreboards and even bilge keels ideally should have a thickness of about 12–15 per cent of their fore and aft length and this maximum width should be about 30 per cent of the length from the nose.

End plates

Basically, end plates are flat bars fitted to but wider than the bottom faces of keels, the top and bottom faces of rudders and so on. They help stop water leaking over from the high pressure to the low pressure side of the structure, causing loss of lift. The famous wing keel on the Australian America's Cup winner was an end plate, amongst other things. Its shape also made it possible to use it as ballast with weight thus concentrated very low down. End plates on keels are rather vulnerable on boats that take the ground.

Propellers on sailing craft

In Chapter 4 some general guidance on propeller diameters was given which can be summed up as that it always pays (from the standpoint of harnessing power efficiently) to use the largest and slowest turning propeller that can be managed. To some extent this dictum is modified to take the speed of the vessel into account and this was covered. However, propellers on sailing vessels are something of a special case, for dragging along a large propeller, designed purely for propulsive efficiency, may cause an unacceptable loss in performance when under sail.

This is a dilemma. To fit a propeller which is too small may mean that in an emergency (just when efficiently harnessed power is needed most) the propeller may be doing little other than beating the water into a froth. Probably the most acceptable solution is to select a propeller diameter that suits the engine fitted with a direct drive gearbox; forget reduction gears. The loss in sailing speed caused by dragging the propeller around may then be around 5 per cent. This drop compares unhappily with the 0.1 drop that might be expected with a folding, centre-line prop. But unless you are quite sure that the engine will never be needed other than for calm water manoeuvring, accept the inevitable.

In round terms, a three-blade propeller is better at pushing a comparatively heavy yacht (heavy, mainly because of its ballast keel) than a two-bladed propeller but the latter causes less drag; a centreline installation is less of an impediment than a wing installation; and a folding type slightly less than a feathering propeller. Unless an exceptionally free-turning shaft/gearbox can be arranged allowing the shaft to freewheel at over about 100 rpm it is generally better to use a shaft brake under sail for reduced drag.

6 Constructional considerations

There are many ways of building a boat, ranging from traditional timber construction in one of its many forms (carvel, clinker and double diagonal amongst them) to its modern derivatives such as cold moulding and strip planking. Then there is ply and, of course, steel and aluminium alloy. Glassfibre (GRP), though probably uneconomic for a 'one-off', is to be seen everywhere and some of its virtues may be translated into foam sandwich construction (GRP skins with a foam core between); this is quite often used on individual boatbuilding projects. Ferro-cement may also be considered where weight does not matter too much and where limited funds are available for hull construction.

Each method of building has its merits and drawbacks which interest a designer and which influence his final choice of material. There will be a brief discussion of such matters in this section. First, though, a few thoughts on the general subject of the likely final weight of the hull. A crude but reasonably effective guide is to work out a skin thickness based on the thickness of a successful example in another material; not forgetting to add in the weight of suitable framing and stiffening as suggested in Chapters 2 and 3.

Suppose, then, that we have gathered from some source that 12 mm ply would be a good skinning material but the designer wants to investigate the possibilities of aluminium alloy and GRP. How thick must each be and how much would it weigh? Use the formula:

$$\text{Thickness}_A = \text{Thickness}_B \times \sqrt[3]{\frac{\text{Modulus}_B}{\text{Modulus}_A}}$$

This raises the question, what is 'modulus'? In fact it is Young's Modulus of elasticity (E) or tensile modulus and a measure of stiffness. Table 3 gave the weight of steel, aluminium alloy, ply, timber and so forth. Parts of this are repeated in Table 15 and extended to suggest the relevant E, or Young's modulus.

So, going back to the formula just given, let us put it to a practical test by assuming that we want to work out a skin thickness equivalent in stiffness to that 12 mm ply. We want figures for aluminium alloy and GRP, with aluminium first:

$$\text{Thickness aluminium} = \text{thickness ply} \times \sqrt[3]{\frac{\text{Modulus ply}}{\text{Modulus aluminium}}}$$

Table 15 Weight and modulus of elasticity of various boatbuilding materials. Normal hardwood planking will have figures quite close to ply's

Material	Weight lb/sq ft/mm (kg/m²/mm)	Young's Modulus 10^6 lbf/in² (10^3/kgf/mm)
Steel	1.6 (7.8)	30 (21)
Aluminium alloy	0.56 (1.73)	10 (7)
GRP	0.3 (1.46)	1.3–1.6 depending on type of laminate (0.9–1.1)
Marine ply	0.14 (0.68)	1.8 (1.2)

Putting in figures:

$$\text{Thickness aluminium} = 12 \times \sqrt[3]{\frac{1.8}{10}}$$
$$\text{Thickness aluminium} = 12 \times 0.56$$

Aluminium thickness = 6.72 mm, or 7 mm near enough.

In Table 15 it will be seen that aluminium alloy weighs 0.56 lb/sq ft/mm thick. So 7 mm plate will weigh 3.92 lb/sq ft.

For the same stiffness 12 mm ply at 0.14 lb/sq ft/mm thick will be 12 × 0.14, or 1.68 lb/sq ft. A clear theoretical victory for ply.

The same sort of sum for 2:1 resin/glass ratio, all-chopped strand mat GRP laminate would go:

$$\text{Thickness GRP} = 12 \times \sqrt[3]{\frac{1.8}{1.3}}$$

Thickness GRP = 13.37 mm. Say, 14 mm.

Glassfibre with a 2:1 resin/glass ratio weighs 0.3 lb/sq ft/mm so that a 14 mm thick laminate will weigh 14 × 0.3 lb/sq ft. That is 4.2 lb/sq ft, so proving to be heavier than either the ply or aluminium, in theory.

Just to clear one thing up when dealing with GRP, weight is usually specified as the weight of glassfibre reinforcement in the laminate only. Thus, a 4 oz laminate has 4 oz/sq ft of glass in it. These days a resin/glass ratio of 2:1 is quite common which means that the 4 oz lay-up will also have 2 × 4, or 8 oz of laminating resin per square foot. This laminate will then actually weigh 12 oz/sq ft but the weight tables in this book have already taken that into consideration.

Just to summarise things so far, Table 16 shows the relative stiffness of rival boatbuilding materials and associated weights. As has been inferred, though, there is more to selecting skin thickness than simply working out relative stiffnesses. Ply, for instance, is not very effective when it comes to impact resistance. Some tests done on different materials showed that with an

Table 16 Actual and relative weights of materials compared with 12 mm marine ply. As in Table 15, hardwoods will be quite close to ply, but some timbers such as fir and ash are likely to be lighter. All figures are based on equivalent stiffness

Material	Weight lb/sq ft (kg/m²)	Relative weight
Steel	7.52 (3.4)	1.00
Aluminium alloy	3.92 (1.76)	0.52
GRP	4.21 (1.89)	0.54
Marine ply	1.68 (0.74)	0.21

impact energy of 9 ft/lb, 18 swg (standard wire gauge) mild steel (2 lb/sq ft) was dented; 14 swg aluminium alloy (1.1 lb/sq ft) was also dented and the panel bent; 6 mm plywood at 0.8 lb/sq ft suffered a fracture of all plies; while two layers of $1\frac{1}{2}$ oz chopped strand mat glassfibre with a 2:1 resin/glass ratio (0.56 lb/sq ft) got away with only slight crazing.

There is a lesson there somewhere which might be that enthusiasm should be tempered by discretion. Stiffness is a good guide but not the only one. Table 16a shows an American study done on a 30 ft, shallow-bodied, fin-keel yacht, 24 ft on the waterline with 10 ft 6 in beam and 5 ft 6 in draught (9.1 m × 7.3 m × 3.2 m × 1.7 m) to determine hull weight, including framing, gave the following results which tend to confirm our league table of comparative weights based on equal stiffness, though with not quite the dramatic differences we managed.

The study did not include steel which would have been the heaviest, or conventional timber building (whose weight would have come out fairly close to steel) while our league table of relative stiffness left out both foam sandwich and traditional construction, there being too many variables in both for them to be useful in such a table.

Now for a brief look at the rival forms of building, beginning with ply.

Table 16a American comparative study on a 30 ft, shallow-bodied, fin-keel yacht (24 ft on waterline, 10.6 in beam, 5 ft 6 in draught)

Material	Construction weight
Aluminium alloy	735 lb (333 kg)
Solid GRP	976 lb (442 kg)
GRP foam core	652 lb (295 kg)
Ply	486 lb (220 kg)
Cold moulded	606 lb (274 kg)

Ply construction

Rather sadly, ply seems to be associated with the cheap and nasty end of the market. Yet good quality marine plywood has been available for many years and, if used properly, has proved to have a long life. There are probably two reasons for its bad reputation. The first is that there has been a flood of poor quality imports claiming to be marine ply and even stamped BS 1088 yet with the core material resembling nothing more than blotting paper. When attacked with a saw, great voids are revealed and considerable areas which are totally bereft of glue. No wonder it has a short life when used as a structural material on a boat.

Marine ply should indeed be to BS 1088 but this has strict rules about the core veneers, which must be virtually to the same specification as the face veneers and both have to be of one of a number of specified tropical hardwoods. Lloyds, in their guidance on the selection of timbers for use as marine plywood, class Agba, Guarea, Idigbo and Utile as being 'durable' while Makore is classed as 'very durable'.

The glue used has to be BS 1203 WBP (weather and boil proof) which makes joints highly resistant to weather, micro-organisms, cold and boiling water, steam and dry heat. The glue used is a phenolic resin. Marine ply produced in this country to BS 1088 is 'kite marked' which implies that it has been inspected during manufacture. Failing this guarantee of quality, ply should be bought that either has an undertaking as to its performance or is personally recommended by someone who knows what he is talking about.

Plywood produced in this country can be obtained in long lengths (up to 30 ft or more) which is often useful. The 4 ft (1220 mm) wide boards are scarphed together at the makers to the length required and these joints, being machine made, are likely to be of a higher standard than those constructed on the workbench.

The second reason for the unpopularity of plywood and its often short life is that not enough attention has been paid to preventing water creeping into exposed raw edges and eventually causing delamination. To some extent this was due to bad design but equally there were no easily available and simple to use materials suitable for the cure. Today, though, the epoxies in their various forms make a very effective water barrier if brushed on exposed edges and used as fillers to work into less than perfect joints.

Epoxies, too, can be used in conjunction with lightweight filler material such as microballoons to form joints. An example would be where they replace the traditional timber chine piece.

Fig 54 shows the midship section of a 15 ft 2 in by 3 ft 6 in (4.6 m × 1.1 m) rowing/sailing skiff (Figs 55 and 56). Here a simple ply construction is used with light battens at chines and deck, more to give a fair edge to the plywood panels than for structural reasons. These edge connections are backed up with glassfibre tape and epoxy resin on the outside of the joint for strength and watertightness. The battens would be glued to the frames, with a gap-filling epoxy mix in the joint opening.

Fig 57 attempts to relate timber planking thickness in inches to the boat's displacement in cubic feet. Remember that a cubic foot of sea water weighs 64 lb and that there are 35 cu ft of sea water to the ton. So if you know the displacement of a boat in pounds or tons you also know its displacement in cubic feet.

Planking thickness may be reduced by about 25 per cent for ply or cold moulded construction.

The dotted lines give an example. Assumed is a boat with 125 cu ft (3.57 tons) displacement. The cube root of 125 is 5.

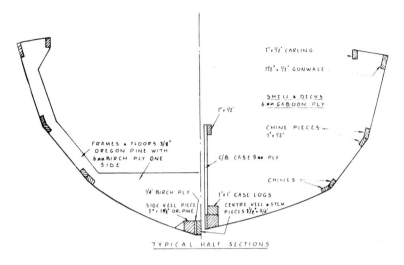

Fig 54   The midship section of a rowing/sailing skiff where epoxy resin and glass tape are used to waterproof and strengthen.

This gives a planking thickness of just over 3/4 in (19 mm) or just over 1/2 in (12 mm) in ply or cold-moulded construction. This thickness is in association with frames at 12 in (300 mm) spacing and which, in this case, have a sectional area of about 2 sq in (1290 mm^2). That means the frames could be something like $1\frac{3}{4}$ in $\times 1\frac{1}{4}$ in (45 mm $\times$ 32 mm) but if the frame spacing is changed, the planking thickness should be changed in proportion. Note that frame area is based on the square root, not cube root of the volumetric displacement.

Cold moulding

Sheet plywood construction is used almost exclusively with hard chine forms. The frames are commonly extended down to the floor (the boat being built upside-down) and the ply panels

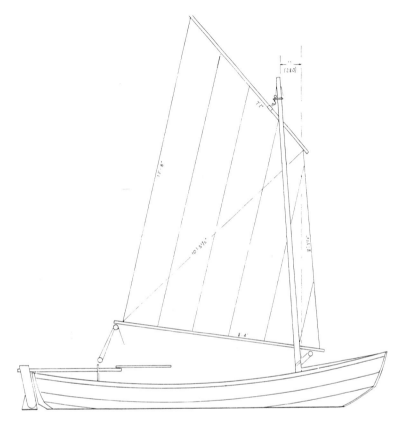

Fig 55   Above water profile of the skiff.

fastened direct to the frames, chine, beam shelf, keel and so on, which are let into those frames.

With cold moulding, temporary frames are set up and clad in closely spaced battens, to form a batten mould. Into this are generally let the keel, stem and, possibly, stern post. The planking is then fastened to the battens, keel and stem; the first, inside layer being isolated from the battens with thin plastic sheet to prevent everything sticking together. There are a minimum of three skins – the first two running diagonally in

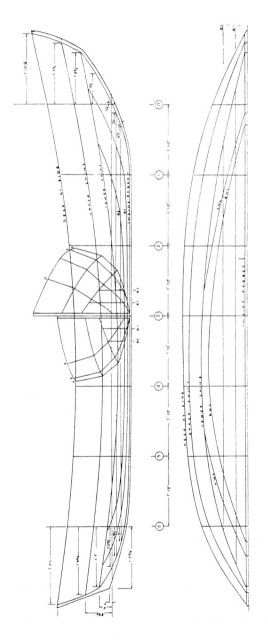

Fig 56   Lines plan of the rowing/sailing skiff.

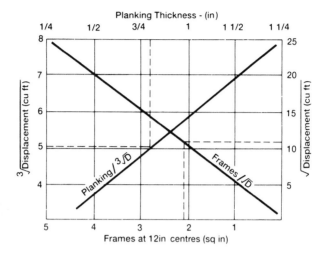

Fig 57   Plank thickness and area of stiffener or frame cross section plotted against the cube root or square root of displacement volume. The figures obtained apply to normal carvel planking but can be modified to suit other planking methods as suggested in the text.

opposite directions with the outside skin lying either fore and aft or diagonally again in the same direction as the first layer. The skins, which may be of ply or veneer strips, are glued together on the mould and when this is done the hull is lifted off the mould complete with keel, stem and so forth, for the frames and bulkheads to be fitted.

Figs 58 and 59 show a profile and lines plan for a 24 ft × 8 ft (7.3 m × 2.4 m) low speed fishing cruiser with a 3/4 in (19 mm) cold moulded hull. An extension of the cold moulding process allows frameless construction to be used if it is considered necessary. What happens is that the hull is first strip-planked over the mould. Strip planks are fairly narrow, run fore and aft and are edge glued. On this structure normal cold moulding is done, glued to the strip planking. This results in a hull at least 7/8 in (22 mm) thick and probably weighing a bit over

118

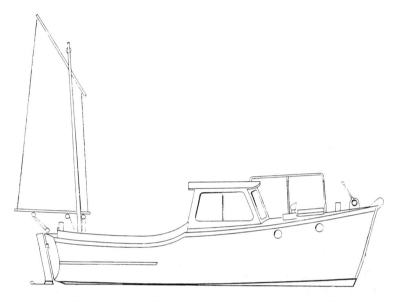

Fig 58   Profile of a small fishing cruiser with a cold-moulded hull.

2 lb/sq ft. Thus it may not be suitable for boats much below 30 ft (9.1 m) in length while it is somewhat labour intensive. Still, a nice uncluttered inside hull surface is something worth taking trouble over. Cold moulding produces a strong, light hull. Like all glued structures it is not easy to repair and having to make a batten mould first is a nuisance.

WEST ^{TM}

The letters stand for 'wood epoxy saturation technique', which is misleading since the epoxy resin that is used encapsulates the timber rather than saturates it. The Gougeon brothers in the USA first developed epoxy resins that would seal wood very effectively and made splendid gap-filling glues. Other companies have also now produced resins to do the same job.

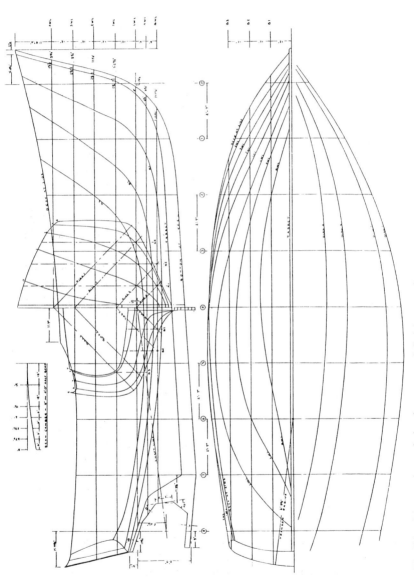

Fig 59   Lines plan of the low speed fishing cruiser.

Timbers such as fir, ash, spruce and cedar have potential strength/weight ratios considerably higher than any rival boat-building materials, with the possible exception of some of the 'exotics' used in conjunction with foam/sandwich construction (see the section on GRP, page 129). For this potential to be realised the wood must have a low moisture content and this can be achieved by first artificially drying the timber to a moisture content of, say, 12 per cent, and then coating it with one of these epoxy resins. Modern paints are good at repelling water but not so effective against water vapour (which is a gas).

The whole structure of the yacht must be thoroughly epoxy-coated inside and out, leaving no bare patches of the type that would occur between frames and planking on a traditionally built vessel. Because greater care can be exercised in ensuring close fitting joints (epoxy glued joints, of course) the WEST℠ system is most commonly found in association with cold moulding.

As the moisture content is low and kept low, the timber does not shrink and swell with every change in the weather (at least not to the same extent as untreated wood) and the chances of rot developing are small.

Traditional timber (with variations)

Cold moulding and ply construction is almost always done with the hull built upside down for ease of working. On conventional construction, though, the boat is more usually worked on right way up; it all depends on the whim of the builder.

With clinker planking where the planks overlap and are fastened together with copper nails and roves (a rove is a kind of washer through which the nail passes and is then cut to the right length and flattened over the rove to form a sort of rivet) the boat's backbone of stem, keel, transom and so forth is set up first together with the building patterns or moulds which define the correct shape. The planking is then done and only now are the frames put in. These are usually timbers of quite small section which, after steaming, are supple enough to be bent into position. They are fastened to the planking with more copper nails and roves. Building moulds are then removed and can be used again if required.

Clinker planking can be about 10 per cent thinner than conventional carvel planking. The resultant boat is thus lighter but because it uses, normally, only small, steamed timbers rather than conventional frames is most suited to vessels under about 30 ft (9.1 m) in length. Minor repairs are straightforward since there are no glued joints but major work demands expert attention. Maintenance tends to be time-consuming, mainly because the interior has many timbers crossing overlapping planking, leaving voids behind which are difficult to clean, let alone paint.

Carvel planking has the individual planks lying flush with each other, the gap between them being filled with caulking cotton and white lead putty (or, today, a synthetic caulking compound). The hull may be framed with steamed timbers as in clinker building or with frames cut or laminated to shape. Very occasionally steel frames are used, in which case the whole thing is known as composite construction.

If sawn or laminated frames are used they are set in place and connected to the keel via their floors before planking starts. In other words the frames take the place of the building moulds but, unlike moulds, are a part of the permanent structure. A traditionally built carvel boat is quite heavy, in weight somewhere between GRP and steel. As with clinker boats minor repairs are quite simple; major work, less so. If carefully built of good materials and subsequently well maintained these traditionally constructed craft have a long life expectancy.

Double diagonal

One variation in planking methods that has a long and honourable history uses double diagonal planking, as demonstrated on all the previous generations of RNLI lifeboats and many of the Second World War torpedo boats. Like clinker work it can be reduced in thickness by about 10 per cent compared with the carvel planking recommendations set out in Fig 57.

As with cold moulded construction the first two layers of planking lie diagonally but in opposite directions. Cold moulding goes on to add a third skin but double diagonal stops at two, and rather than being glued together the layers are fastened together with copper nails and roves with the planking sandwiching a layer of unbleached calico soaked in white lead paint. This must still be wet when the planks are riveted together. The calico covers the gaps which occur at each plank crossing. Steamed timbers are normally employed to give a strong, flexible hull which uses, advantageously, comparatively short lengths of planking. Repairs tend to be difficult and eventually when the calico/white lead paint dries out this waterproofing layer may start to leak; such leaks are very difficult to cure.

Strip and long diagonal planking

These are both schemes where the plank edges are glued together with the result that, though they are strong, they are also difficult to repair. With strip planking, quite narrow planks run fore and aft. Edges may be bevelled to give a close fit or one edge on each plank is rounded, the other hollowed, thus allowing one to sit in the other, eliminating the need for bevelling on most planks. This rounding and hollowing would be done by woodworking machinery, not by hand on the bench. Especially where strip planking round a tight turn, fastenings are used down through the planks to pull them together. These may be nails, or wood dowels about 1/8 in diameter.

As an alternative to bevelling or rounding, square edge planks may be used, keeping the edges tight on the inside and subsequently filling the resultant gap on the outside with a low density epoxy filler.

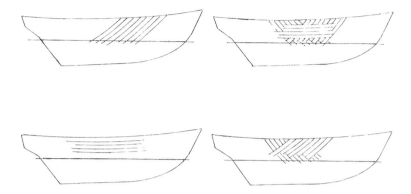

Fig 60 The run of planking in different building methods. Going clockwise from the top, left-hand sketch are: long diagonal; triple skin cold moulding; double diagonal; and strip planking.

Long diagonal planking employs a single skin, running diagonally (Fig 60). Basically the method of working is to butt succeeding planks against one another; run a spindle up the jointing faces to cut away the wood for a perfect fit; then push one plank against the other and glue the edges. Like double diagonal work, this system needs only comparatively short lengths of planking. Again planks can be through fastened in awkward areas.

Steel

Steel is undeniably heavy and in thicknesses below $\frac{1}{8}$ in (3 mm) is very prone to distortion when welding. Since 3 mm plate weighs some 5 lb/sq ft (24.5 kg/m^2) it will not be much use for any boat under about 25 ft (7.6 m) in length. Yet it is strong and stiff; if your steel-hulled cruiser was to be carried on to a coral reef, it might buckle and distort but it is likely to remain watertight when other materials have shattered. It is also fairly easy to effect temporary repairs by welding on a patch. If built under cover using shot-blasted and primed steel it will have a long, low-maintenance life. Further blasting can be done on damaged and welded areas before final priming with any of the excellent coatings available today – epoxies amongst them. If built in the open, then shot blasting should be done to the bare steel at the last stage and should be primed as quickly as possible (within a few hours). Pre-primed steel is not then particularly useful as it tends to deteriorate in the weather and show unwelcome rusty patches. So the whole boat, inside and out, will need shot blasting anyway.

The fact that it is difficult to use steel of thicknesses under 3 mm has been mentioned and this can lead to problems on small yachts and motor sailers with extensive steel superstructures, wheelhouses and the like. Normally in boatbuilding, the designer tries to arrange things so that the higher above the waterline a structure is, the thinner or lighter are the materials used. This, of course, is to aid stability (more on this in Chapter 7) by keeping the vertical centre of gravity (vcg) as low as possible. But if one is stuck with 3 mm steel there is not much that can be achieved in that direction. On these craft, then, it is often sensible to consider superstructures in ply or aluminium alloy.

To do this, a steel flat bar is welded round the periphery of the upperworks, inclined in from the vertical by an amount to match the tumblehome of the superstructure. To this is bolted the ply and its timber stiffeners.

In the case of aluminium, there should be an insulating tape between the steel bar and aluminium plate. Bolts can be galvanised steel or stainless steel. If made of stainless steel, they should be fitted through sleeves of an inert material, like nylon, with inert washers under the heads and nuts. This is to prevent electrolytic action between the steel and alloy which would eat away the aluminium.

Table 17 shows the galvanic series with the noble or cathodic metals at the top. They will tend to attack the base or anodic metals towards the bottom and the further apart they are in the table the more vicious will be the action in sea water. Stainless steel appears twice. This is because it normally forms

Table 17 The galvanic series. Those at the noble end will attack those at the base end when in close proximity in sea water

Noble or cathodic end	
Stainless steel type 316	Lead
Stainless steel type 304	Stainless steel with oxide destroyed
Stainless steel type 321	Cast iron
Monel	Mild steel
Gunmetal	Aluminium alloys
Phosphor bronze	Cadmium plating
Admiralty brass	Galvanised steel
Red brass	Zinc
Copper	Magnesium
Naval brass	**Base or anodic end**
Manganese bronze	

a protective film round itself (like aluminium alloy) but should that be destroyed, as might be the case, for instance, where stainless steel is used as a propeller shaft and the underwater bearing through which it passes wears off the protective film, it drops down the galvanic series towards the base end. It is obvious, incidentally, why zinc anodes are used. Practically every other metal will attack it in preference to metals which might be structurally essential. Magnesium anodes are normally used in fresh water.

Returning to steel construction, integral fuel tanks save space and money. They need big manholes in them so that inspection and maintenance can be carried out. Water tanks should be made of stainless or aluminium alloy; water is considerably more corrosive to steel than diesel fuel.

The specification of steel used in boatbuilding is usually BS 4360 43A, which is a conventional mild steel. Special steels such as Corten, which has a low carbon content but additional copper and manganese, are sometimes used but, in general, their greater cost and possible welding difficulties rule them out.

Some suggested skin thicknesses are given in the sections on timber and GRP, but thicknesses for steel have not been attempted since plate thicknesses are largely governed by what is commercially available. It would be no use, for example, working out that a craft of 5 tons displacement required 3.6 mm plating, since this specification is unavailable.

What can be said in general terms is that below 30 ft (9.1 m), 3 mm plating for bottom, sides and decks might be appropriate with something like 65 mm ×50 mm ×6 mm ($2\frac{1}{2}$ in × 2 in × $\frac{1}{4}$ in) frames at about 3 ft 3 in (1 m) centres. From 30–40 ft (9.1–12.2 m) length, 4 mm bottom and side plating might be used with 3 mm decks. Frames could be increased to 75 mm ×50 mm × 6 mm (3 in × 2 in × $\frac{1}{4}$ in) at that 3 ft 3 in spacing. Above 40 ft we are moving towards 6 mm bottom plating with 4 mm topsides and decks. Frames might now be 80 mm ×60 mm ×6 mm ($3\frac{1}{2}$ in × $2\frac{1}{2}$ in × $\frac{1}{4}$ in) on the same centres as before which fit in quite well with an accommodation bulkhead spacing of 2 m. None of these suggestions reduces the need to consult the rules of the classification societies (such as Lloyds) if the job is to be done properly. Their purpose is simply to give the designer some idea of what he is letting himself in for.

Apart from, maybe, a collision bulkhead forward, steel bulkheads are best avoided in small craft. They are heavy and tend to be wavy, needing cladding if they are to look reasonable. Ply bulkheads are generally preferable. In bigger boats there might be steel bulkheads forward and aft of the engine compartment. It is easy to make steel bulkheads watertight.

Figs 61 and 62 show the lines and list of scantlings for a 55 ft junk-rigged ketch. There is nothing of very great note except that chine bars have been used. These are not strictly necessary but some builders like them both to prevent chafing damage at what might be considered vulnerable corners if the plates were simply butted up and welded (as is quite common) and to give a fair curve to the chine. Their drawback is that twice as many welding runs have to be made than if the side and bottom plates were butted.

Welding on steel boats may be normal electric arc (versatile and economical) or by one of the shielded arc processes where the arc is shrouded in an inert gas such as CO. This latter method produces less distortion, is somewhat more expensive and rather unsuitable for building in the open where wind can disturb the shielding gas.

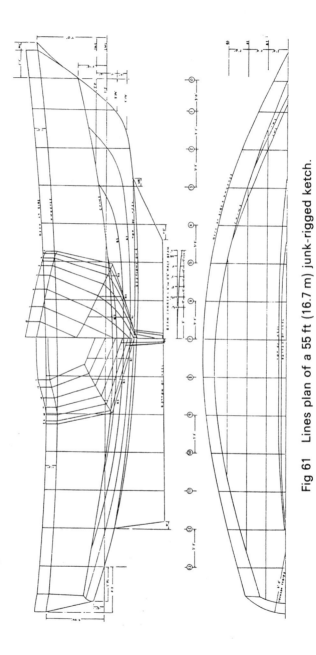

Fig 61   Lines plan of a 55 ft (16.7 m) junk-rigged ketch.

Scantlings

Bottom of keel	9 mm
Keel sides	6 mm
Bottom shell	5 mm
Side shell	5 mm
Decks and cockpit sole	4 mm
Floors	6 mm
Bulkheads	4 mm
Brackets	6 mm with 8 in arms
Face bar	65 mm × 6 mm
Gunwale bar	5 in O.D. tube
Chine bar	3 in O.D. tube or 100 × 9 F.B.
Stem bar	100 mm × 12 mm F.B.
Hull frames	130 mm × 6 mm F.B.
Deck beams	80 mm × 6 mm F.B.
Bulkhead stiffs	65 mm × 6 mm F.B.
Pillars	65 mm × 4 mm tube on alternate beams
Hull stringers	65 mm × 6 mm F.B.
Deck stringers	40 mm × 6 mm F.B.
Engine beds	6 mm

Fig 62   List of the principal steel scantlings from the same 55 ft ketch.

Aluminium alloy

Most boats are built (in much the same way as steel) of alloys such as NE5 or NE8 for extrusions, NS5 or NS8 for sheet and so on. These are weldable alloys but welding must be by a shielded arc process.

Like steel, aluminium can distort while welding and something like 3/16 in ($4\frac{1}{2}$ mm) plate is the minimum thickness that can be welded with the expectation of distortion-free completion.

Aluminium, having a Young's Modulus of 10 as compared with steel's 30×10^6, needs to be about 1.5 times as thick as steel for equal strength and will then weigh about half as much, so it is a very worthwhile, though somewhat expensive, boat-building material.

All sorts of scaremongering goes on when aluminium is discussed, often with the inference that it will simply melt away given half a chance and cannot be fitted out using normal materials. This is simply not the case. Aluminium or plastic seacocks can replace the traditional bronze types; galvanised mild steel is very close to aluminium in the galvanic series table and so can be used for keel and other bolts; a stainless steel propeller shaft is automatically isolated from any alloy structure by its bearing material; a bronze propeller can be hard chrome plated if there are any worries on that score; and so on.

In fact if steel can be considered a low maintenance material when properly prepared and coated, aluminium alloys provide a no-maintenance structure. There is no need to paint them, apart from decorative and anti-fouling considerations, as they form a protective film over the surface which will form again if destroyed locally. Effective repairs may be difficult in out-of-the-way places where the correct welding gear and alloys of the right specification are conspicuous by their absence.

Ferro-concrete

Not so long ago people turned to ferro-concrete when funds were short and ambition high for it is possible to build a largish cruiser in this material for considerably less money than any other. The work involved is grindingly hard but no special skills are needed except right at the end of the building process when the concrete has to be worked through the armature of chicken wire, tubes and rods to form a smooth, fair skin inside and out without voids or air entrapment. Still, professionals can be hired to undertake this work and since it should be completed in a day the cost is not too great.

Unhappily, the hull represents only a comparatively small part of the total cost of a boat and many unfinished yachts dot our coastline as a sad testimony to this fact. Ferro-concrete boats other than those built by one or two well known yards tend to have a low re-sale value. This is not because there is anything intrinsically wrong with the material – there isn't – but it is difficult for people to judge the quality of the workmanship after the boat has been completed. What voids lurk under that shiny exterior, perhaps leading to possible corrosion and strength problems? Indeed, does the paint conceal the fact that the reinforcing is perilously close to the surface with almost inevitable rusting and then wholesale corrosion with the concrete cracking as a result? Even a surveyor will find it hard to tell.

Ferro-concrete boats cannot rot, be attacked by worms or suffer from osmosis but they are heavy, generally weighing slightly more than a steel hull. Though sometimes additives are put in the cement mix to delay curing (important in hot weather) or to reduce water requirements, most often simple Portland cement is used with a water/cement ratio of about $0:35$ with $3\frac{1}{2}$ gallons (16 litres) of water to each 112 lb (50 kg) bag of cement. The sand/cement ratio is about $2:1$ by weight.

There are two principal methods of construction. The first is to set the hull up on the boat's frames (generally steel pipe) as in traditional timber or steel construction. Keel, stem and so forth are also pipe while all these are supplemented by numerous round bar longitudinals. Several layers of chicken wire or similar steel mesh are lashed to this framework with twists of wire, and bound together by the same method. Everything is smoothed and faired to give an accurate hull shape and the cement mix is then worked through and vibrated with mechanical vibrators to reduce air entrapment. The second building scheme is to set up a batten mould as in cold moulded construction and erect the hull on that. Though this makes for easier fairing the dangers of pockets of air being left in the concrete are increased.

The finished hull is often draped in sacking and intermittently sprayed with water for a week or so to delay curing. Finally it is painted with a good waterproofing paint, such as an epoxy.

GRP

Though glassfibre reinforced plastic (GRP) is by far the most common boatbuilding material today that does not imply that it is necessarily the best. It is simply a good all-round medium, admirably suited to limited production runs. It does not rot, though it may develop osmosis; and it does not corrode though it burns spectacularly well unless fire retardant resins are used. These tend to be expensive and do not weather as well as those commonly used.

A GRP boat is made by bonding together in a mould several layers of glassfibre with, generally, a polyester resin. The glassfibre comes in several guises, the principal of which are chopped strand mat and woven rovings. Both are made from glass heated to some 1300–1400 °C in an electric furnace and then rapidly drawn through platinum bushings to be bundled together to form a strand. The strands are next either combined to form chopped strand mat, made from 1–2 in (25–50 mm) strands held together in a random manner by a resinous binder; or woven into a plain, square pattern to become woven rovings.

Chopped strand mat is comparatively cheap and forms the basis of most boat laminates. It is simple to work the resin through successive glass layers to build up the required thickness but used alone it lacks stiffness, especially if the resin content is too high. A 3:1 resin/glass ratio could lead to an E figure as low as 0.8. On many hulls, then, chopped strand mat is combined with alternate layers of the stronger woven rovings to produce E figures of as high as 1.8. The resin/glass ratio should be around 2:1.

One has to start somewhere with not too many variables, so laminate weight recommendations are normally made on a basis of chopped strand mat alone, as is Fig 63. This works with the boat's displacement as a basis. The dotted lines plot the course for a vessel where the cube root of the displacement in cubic feet is 5 (so displacement is 5^3, or 125 cu ft). The weight of the bottom laminate would then be about 8 oz of chopped strand mat and stiffeners would be spaced at 19 in centres. If woven rovings were incorporated, Young's modulus, E, might go up from 1.3 to 1.6, whereupon the bottom laminate could be reduced by the method touched on earlier.

Conventionally, GRP boats are built by first making an exact replica of the vessel in some stable timber (this replica being

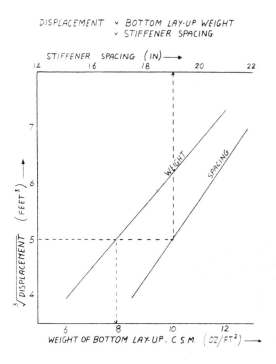

Fig 63 Suggested weight of bottom laminate (in chopped strand mat with a 2:1 resin/glass ratio) and stiffener spacing based on the cube root of the volumetric displacement.

known as the plug); then taking a mould off it; and finally laminating inside the mould. This is clearly uneconomic for a 'one-off', but a substitute constructional scheme is on offer. This is to make a batten mould first, as in cold moulding, and then to cover this in a layer of rigid-cell expanded plastic such as expanded polyurethane. The foam is temporarily fastened to the mould and sheathed in GRP. It is then lifted off and sheathed on the inside with another layer of GRP. Subsequently the inevitably rather rough finish inside and out is smoothed and faired. This represents a lot of hard work.

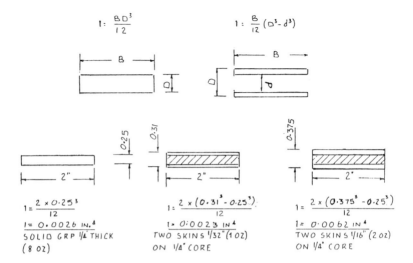

Fig 64   The method of working out the main ingredients of a foam sandwich laminate of equal strength to one of solid GRP.

Fig 64 shows how to work out the weight of laminate in foam core or sandwich building (the method described above) to equal the strength of a solid laminate. If the latter was an 8 oz lay-up (about $\frac{1}{4}$ in thick) and it was intended to use a $\frac{1}{4}$ in (6 mm) thick foam core in sandwich construction, just for the sake of argument, you would first work out the moment of inertia (I) of the solid example, taking a piece of the bottom of some arbitrary width. Here 2 in was taken but any width would do. That answer was 0.0026 in⁴.

What we are aiming for is to find an I figure using the foam core and a layer of glass and resin on each side that equals, or is greater than, the figure for the solid laminate. So now we can have a go with the thinnest possible GRP lay-up of 1 oz, which is 1/32 in thick, both sides. The internal depth is still 0.25 in but outside it is now $\frac{1}{4}$ in +1/16 in, or 0.31 in. Thus I is 0.0023 in⁴, which is too low, thank goodness, for that would have been a pretty feeble affair with the outer skins too thin to resist much abrasion. Do the sum again, but this time with double the skin thickness and the answer is a satisfactory

134

moment of inertia figure of $0.0062\,\text{in}^4$, with the hull then weighing considerably less than one of a solid laminate. Expanded foam can be taken as weighing something in the order of 4–7 lb/cu ft (64–$112\,\text{kg/m}^3$).

The usual glass reinforcing in a laminate is E glass with an ultimate tensile strength of about 500 000 lb/sq in. In high stress areas of the hull, and to stiffen up longitudinals, even stronger reinforcing can be used, at the expense of generally more difficult 'wetting out' with the resin and inevitably higher cost. One such reinforcing is S-glass with two other better known types being carbon fibre and Kevlar. The latter is generally used in woven roving form while carbon fibre is employed mainly as a unidirectional roving to strengthen stringers and frames. It is also found in the production of unstayed masts where its stiffness is a valuable asset. Some weight is saved by using these 'exotic' reinforcings but it is impossible to generalise.

The usual unsaturated polyester laminating resin can be replaced by epoxy resin or, as a half-way house between the two, vinylester resin. Both are more expensive than the polyesters but both provide better strength, adhesion and waterproofing qualities.

7 Stability

Stability is a subject where a little knowledge is useful but more than that is unnecessary. Designers only occasionally get asked to do stability calculations, and if they are, there are learned bodies equipped with computers programmed to do the very tedious and lengthy sums. If the designer can supply the computer with the information it needs and can then understand the results produced he will have done his part.

All stability calculations revolve around knowing the positions of, first, the centre of gravity, G, and second, the centre of buoyancy, B. In past calculations we worked out the location of the longitudinal centre of gravity (lcg) by taking moments about midships. Now we could extend the process by taking moments of the same items of hull structure and equipment but this time above and below the load waterline (lwl). Divide the total moments by the total weight as before and the result would be a vertical location for G. That is the principal item of information needed by the computer but leaves unresolved a location for B.

However much a boat heels it is assumed that G remains in the same place, as indeed it will as long as nothing breaks loose and the vessel does not flood. B, though, being the centre of area of the underwater volume must shift with every different angle of heel as it moves to become the centre of the changed under-water area. The work involved in calculating this new position for many different angles of heel is lengthy, as can be imagined, and best left to the wizardry of the computer.

In all cases the weight of the vessel acts vertically down through the centre of gravity, G, while the boat's buoyancy, an equal and opposite force, acts vertically up through B. They must be equal and opposite for if B were mysteriously the greater the vessel would rise bodily in the water. If G were greater the opposite would occur.

Sketch 1 of Fig 65 shows a mythical yacht in repose. The locations of G and B are marked. Sketch 2 has the boat heeling to about 25 deg. G remains in its previous position, on the centreline and at a certain height above the keel but B has moved across to become the centre of area of the new, heeled underwater shape.

Where the vertical through B cuts the yacht's centreline is marked M, which is called the **metacentre** and the distance from G to M is the metacentric height. This is a measure of stability but a better one is the length of the righting arm, GZ. That is called the righting lever and is often used in stability diagrams, of which more will be said in a moment. If the length of the line GZ had been multiplied by the boat's displacement in tons, pounds, kilograms or what you will, the result would be termed a **righting moment**.

Returning to sketch 2, it can be seen that the opposing forces through G and B are acting to twist the boat back upright and thus are acting as what is termed a **righting couple**. It is worth noting that if G had been located at a greater height above the keel than the position shown, GM would have been less, GZ shorter and the righting couple less powerful. A boat of the same form as the one shown but with less ballast or heavier upperworks or beefier spars or, possibly, a lighter engine would have a higher G, to give a more sluggish response to heeling.

Sketches 3 and 4 follow the vessel round at increasing angles of heel (78 deg and 150 deg). In both cases M is still above G and there are still righting couples, though only just in the last

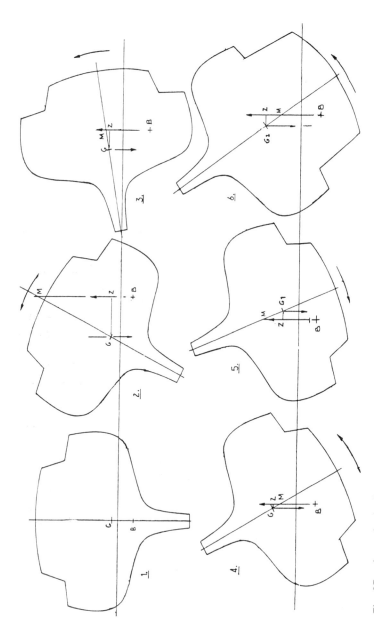

Fig 65 A yacht hull at various angles of heel showing the positions of the centres of gravity and buoyancy (G and B) in all cases.

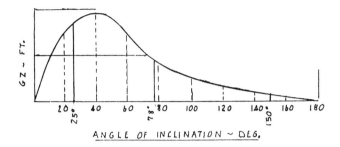

Fig 66   Curves of righting levers (GZ) plotted against angles of heel for the yacht in Fig 65.

case. If that can be sustained for a few degrees more the craft will be able to right herself from any angle of heel and would be known as a self-righter.

In Fig 66 these and other righting levers (GZ) in feet or metres are plotted against angles of keel and this is known as a **stability curve** or a curve of righting levers.

Back again to Fig 65. Sketch 5 has the boat heeled to about 150 deg as in sketch 4 but with a raised position of G, which is shown as G_1, just to demonstrate what happens when G is allowed to climb too high. Now M is below G_1 and what was a positive righting couple, GZ, has been transformed into a cap-sizing couple. The opposing forces through G_1 and B are acting to turn the boat well and truly upside down. This is what happens on the majority of boats; at some angle of heel the forces change sides and conspire to invert the vessel.

In sketch 6 the same hull as before has had a large superstruc-ture added and the centre of gravity, now G_2, has risen in consequence. There is still a righting couple, however, because the vessel is floating partly on her superstructure, with B in a new and advantageous position. This is the scheme used on some RNLI lifeboats to make them self-righting. A large, watertight deckhouse does the trick but must be combined with auto-matically closing vents and engine intakes. So perhaps there is something to be said for capacious wheelhouses, apart from being able to take tea and biscuits out of the wind and rain. Air bags strapped to the highest point of a hull or superstructure perform the same function. On inflation they persuade the boat to float so high in the water when inverted as to become a self-righter.

It looks, then, from our efforts so far, that a low centre of gravity is a good thing and, in fact, comparing two similar vessels but with different G heights, the one with the lower G will normally have a greater maximum righting lever and will also have a greater range of stability. That is, even if not a self-righter she will still right herself from larger angles of heel.

The same applies to raising the freeboard. High freeboard, however undesirable for windage and whether caused by high topsides or high deckworks, does marvels for maximum righting moments and range of stability. That is unless G is allowed to rise too much in sympathy. Keep deckhouses and so forth as light as possible, commensurate with adequate strength.

What about beam? How does this affect things? Fig 67 is meant to bring a little light to bear. It shows the curves of

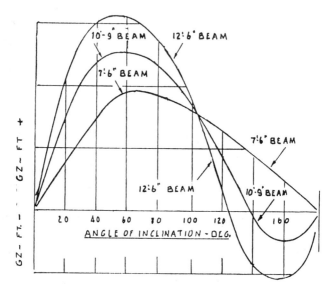

Fig 67 Three 33 ft (10 m) yachts of different beam showing the effect this has on stability. Only the narrowest is a self-righter.

righting levers for three yachts all 33 ft (10 m) in length and with 4.5 tons displacement but with beams of 12 ft 6 in (3.8 m), 10 ft 9 in (3.3 m) and 7 ft 9 in (2.4 m). Note that the curves extend below the base line for the two widest yachts. As discussed, just as there are positive righting levers trying to restore a vessel to an upright stance, there are negative righting, or capsizing levers, where the action is to invert the boat totally. That is what levers below the base are doing. It will be clear that the greater the beam the 'stiffer' the yacht will be with good righting levers initially. Thus with 12 ft 6 in beam the righting lever, GZ, at 60 degrees heel is over 3 ft; with 10 ft 9 in beam this has dropped to some 2 ft 6 in; and at 7 ft 9 in beam it is less than 2 ft. This is what we would expect, but look at the capsizing angles where GZ becomes negative and is working to capsize the vessel. The widest beam boat will capsize if heeled to angles over about 125 degrees and so will the 10 ft 9 in beam yacht at angles over, roughly, 140 deg, while the narrowest craft will have a positive, restoring lever at all angles of heel. G is assumed to be at the same height on all models.

This is the normal pattern of events. All other things being equal, a beamy boat will be stiffer than a comparable narrow rival and better able to stand up to a press of sail without excessive heel. But in the last analysis and a total knock-down the slimmer vessel is likely to right herself whereas the beamier craft may remain capsized and upside-down.

All stability calculations assume that the hull and superstructure remain watertight at all times and angles of heel. The odd dribble of water past hatchboards or through a not-quite-closed vent won't upset things unduly but an open hatch or door will most probably ensure that any potential the yacht had for self-righting is destroyed.

In the wake of several spectacular capsizes by prominent yachtsmen taking part in ocean racing has come an upsurge of interest in stability, and ways to assess it without going to the trouble and expense of doing full stability calculations.

One such suggestion is that if the following formula works out to give a figure of 2.0 or over, the yacht involved could be considered to be potentially unsafe offshore.

$$\frac{\text{Maximum beam in feet}}{\sqrt[3]{\text{displacement in } \dfrac{\text{lb}}{64}}}$$

Taking an average sort of yacht, say 35 ft (10.7 m) on the waterline where beam might be 12 ft and displacement 7 tons, the sum becomes:

$$\frac{12}{\sqrt[3]{7 \times 2240/64}} \text{ which is } \frac{12}{6.25} \text{ or } 1.92$$

So she is just about suitable for offshore work.

Stability criteria can be taken one step forward from generalities, where we left them, to some form of practicality by using Blom's experimental method (which is not too complicated).

Cut a set of full sections (not half-sections) at various angles of heel from thin card. These might be 30 degrees, 60 degrees and 90 degrees. The shape of each set can be lifted off the body plan. Leave a fair margin above the inclined waterline for subsequent trimming.

Cut a further set of sections for the vessel in the upright condition. On all sets the centreline and LWL should be marked. Each set should now be glued together using a thin coating of uniform thickness glue with the sections in their right order and with centrelines and LWLs properly aligned. Each set is then pared down parallel to the waterline with a sharp knife until it weighs the same as the upright, no heel, set. Displacement is then the same for each set, as it must be in practice on the full size boat.

Next suspend each set from their opposite corners and mark the line given by a plumb bob from both corners. The intersection of those lines shows the position of the centre of gravity of the set, which is also the centre of buoyancy, B. Put a vertical up through this point and where it intersects the centreline will be M, the metacentre. The method for finding G, the vertical centre of gravity was explained near the beginning of this section on stability. A vertical dropped from G will cut the line from B to M at some point, Z. GZ is then the righting lever and it can be scaled off each set of sections to give the figure for that particular angle of heel. A curve of righting levers can then be constructed which will be quite tolerably accurate, and should demonstrate the angle at which the boat will theoretically capsize.

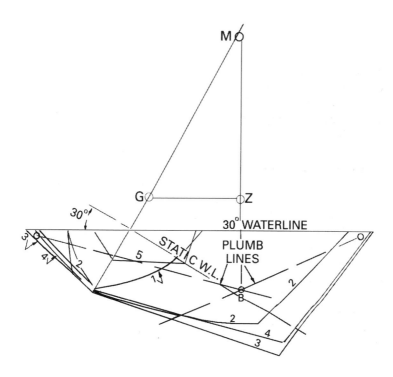

Fig 67a   Blom's experimental method of finding the vertical centre of buoyancy, righting lever and metacentric height, GM, on a double chine hull inclined at 30 degrees.

8 Further design considerations

Finally, some rather random thoughts on subjects which cannot really be classed as boat designing but which come into the reckoning when pursuing that activity. Accommodation, for instance; if drawing out a cruising boat it is a little disappointing, to say the least, to discover late on in the proceedings that the hoped-for layout simply won't fit in the otherwise splendid hull that reposes on the drawing board.

Accommodation

Ideas should be sketched out on the first rough lines plan just to check that all is potentially well. Think also about the siting of principal bulkheads at this stage. They should fall either well clear of frames – otherwise it may prove difficult to fit them – or on a frame which they can replace or be attached to; the latter being common practice on steel and aluminium alloy construction when ply bulkheads are used.

The first act in planning a layout is to draw the cabin sole line on the lines plan at what appears a sensible height. From this a cabin sole width can be found, bearing in mind that such things as frames can encroach quite significantly on apparently available space. Following on from the sole, sketch in bunk and work-top heights and widths, again thinking of frames.

If things get too difficult the sole can be swept up towards the bow to take advantage of the fact that the higher the sole is, the wider it will be, and that the deck is probably sweeping up also, so that no headroom is lost. This curved-in-profile sole is preferable to having steps, over which people will trip at sea. The sole can also be mildly concave in section to allow more headroom over its lowest point.

Work tops should be about 3 ft (0.9 m) above the sole and berths can be as little as 2 ft (0.6 m) wide at the shoulders tapering to 1 ft 6 in (0.45 m) at the foot. For adults they should be at least 6 ft 6 in (2 m) long. Where there are upper and lower bunks or in the case of quarter berths there should be not less than 1 ft 9 in (0.53 m) turning-over room above the mattress. Two feet (0.6 m) of clear passage is needed between obstructions such as work surfaces, lockers and bulkheads. Study chandlers' catalogues for sizes of cookers, sinks, toilets, handbasins and so forth and avoid the common pitfall of siting handbasins under side decks. Admittedly they take up little room there, which is just as well since they are also quite useless.

Fig 68 shows some sitting heights at various angles of inclination. Thus if one is almost recumbent you can get away with only about 3 ft 2 in (0.96 m) headroom under the deck, but if using a table for eating, more like 4 ft 8 in (1.42 m) is needed. The third sketch shows another possibility; note that the height to the top of the settee cushion and the slope of the backrest have to be different for each selection.

Obviously the best way to study accommodation layouts is have a look at existing boats or, failing that, to peruse the accommodation plans that frequently appear in the boating journals. As a general rule, try not to be too ambitious. A simple, uncluttered accommodation is generally to be preferred to the fussy and crowded.

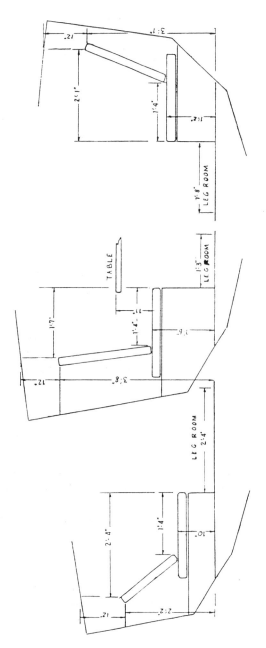

Fig 68   Minimum sitting headroom is governed by the height of the settee above the sole and the angle of its backrest.

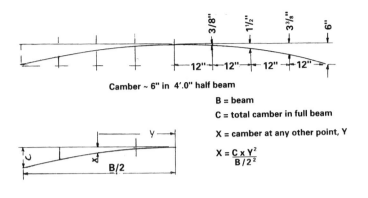

Camber ~ 6" in 4'.0" half beam

B = beam

C = total camber in full beam

X = camber at any other point, Y

$$X = \frac{C \times Y^2}{B/2^2}$$

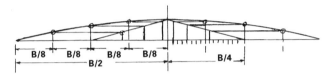

PARABOLIC CAMBER

Fig 69 Two methods of drawing out the camber curve. The top one shows a mathematical scheme. The other is more of an exercise in drawing but produces equally good results.

Camber

There are at least four ways of drawing out the camber curve to which the upper face of a deck beam is cut. A curved beam promotes stiffness in the deck, sheds water quickly and allows greater headroom below without having to raise the cabin sides, which is the alternative. Here are two ways.

Method one is a mathematical scheme. Use the formula:

$$X = \frac{C}{(B/2)^2} \times Y^2$$

To find X, the round-down of the beam at any point, Y; knowing the beam of the craft and the total camber. For example, 4 in camber in 7 ft beam or, in the case illustrated, 6 in camber in 8 ft total beam. Putting figures in:

$$X = \frac{6}{4^2} \times 2^2 = 1.5 \text{ in}$$

assuming that we wanted to know the round-down at 2 ft beam.

At 1.5 ft beam, round-down would be:

$$X = \frac{6}{4^2} \times 1.5^2 = 0.84 \text{ in}$$

The second method is as follows. Subdivide the beam of the boat into two equal parts about its centreline. Mark the desired camber on the vertical through the half beam. Next subdivide the quarter beam into sixteen equal parts and draw a diagonal line from the desired camber on the vertical down to the quarter beam division. Using those sixteen subdivisions, erect verticals through divisions 1, 4 and 9 and square them up to the diagonal line. At these intersections horizontals are drawn to the one-eighth beam divisions. Draw in the curve that fits those points and there is the camber curve. Fig 69 illustrates both schemes. The latter is not as complicated as it seems, on paper.

Stanchions and bulwarks

For peace of mind at sea, bulwarks come high on the list of priorities. They can be as low as 1 ft (0.3 m) and still be very effective solid water and human barriers. At the same time they allow stanchions to be much more securely fastened than is normally possible on GRP and timber boats. With steel and alloy vessels, of course, stanchions can be welded directly to the deck which would have to tear up before the stanchions gave way.

Bulwarks
Bulwarks must not be allowed to hold water on deck; so they need openings cut in them. Lloyds give the following formula for the area of opening in m^2 per side. This applies to deck

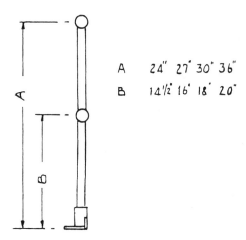

A   24" 27" 30" 36"

B   14½" 16" 18" 20"

Fig 70   Stanchions may be epoxy-painted or galvanised mild steel; aluminium alloy; or stainless steel. Don't deride mild steel. It is cheap, strong and simply fabricated.

scuppers, scupper pipes and cockpit drains, assuming that the bulwarks form a well, as a cockpit does:

$$A = 0.01 \times l \times h + 0.035 \times l \times h^2$$

where A is the area of opening per side in m^2; l is the length of the bulkwark (or cockpit) in metres; h is the height of the bulwark (or depth of cockpit) in metres. So if a bulwark was, say, 9 m long and its depth was 0.5 m, the required area of deck scupper per side would be:

$$A = 0.01 \times 9 \times 0.5 + 0.035 \times 9 \times 0.5^2$$

$$= 0.045 + 0.079$$

$$= 0.124 \ m^2 \ or \ 1.33 \ sq \ ft \ or \ 191.5 \ sq \ in$$

This area could be arranged as a gap between the bottom of the bulwark and deck edge over its whole length or in the form of freeing ports spread along the length.

Stanchions
Stanchions may be spaced as far apart as 6 ft (1.8 m) but are better at about 4 ft (1.2 m) when they are stronger and follow

the contours of the deck edge more closely. Fig 70 shows typical stanchion heights together with appropriate heights of the centre eye. A stanchion as low as 2 ft (0.6 m) is a poor affair, 2 ft 3 in (0.7 m) being really the practical minimum.

Rake of masts

All masts should rake aft for appearance's sake. On two- (or three-)masted rigs the forward mast should be the most upright, with those further aft having successively greater rake, otherwise it appears that they are leaning in towards each other. Great rake, though looking attractive on some rigs, means that when running in light airs the booms tend to swing inboard which can be a nuisance. Single-masted rigs can rake about 1:35 while on ketches, yawls and the like the mainmast might have a rake of something like 1:25.

In conclusion

As I put together my final thoughts in this chapter, I am haunted by thoughts of 'What other aspects or further information could I have added?' But I hope that I have given the interested reader enough basic information to enable him or her to start their own projects and work through a design to the point where good performance under sail or power is reasonably assured. Further reading should fill in the finer points of detail.

Yacht design has become a rather high-tech business these days with designers using computers to aid their skills. Yet they are merely working through the same design processes as are described in this book – more swiftly and expensively but probably with no finer results than the designer crouched over a drawing board with a pad of paper and simple calculator by his side.

So if you do feel inspired to design your own boat, go ahead and give it a try. You will derive immense satisfaction and interest from the project. Just remember: be as accurate as possible with your measurements and calculations and keep your design simple.

Glossary

Angle of entrance The angle the forward waterlines make with the centreline at their forward ends. Generally the angle of the load waterline (lwl) is used for comparison purposes.

Area curve See **curve of areas.**

Aspect ratio As applied to sails, rudders and centreboards, it is the length of the leading edge (the luff when referring to sails) squared, divided by the area of the sail, rudder or what-have-you. Generally a high aspect ratio rudder, for instance, is more efficient than one with a lower ratio.

Block coefficient The ratio of the immersed volume of the hull to the products of length, beam and draught of the circumscribing block. That is $C_b = \dfrac{Disp. \times 35}{L \times B \times D}$ for salt water. Displacement is in tons and other dimensions in feet. For fresh water 35.9 is used rather than 35 in the top line.

Block coefficient may be used for a preliminary estimate of draught. The higher the coefficient, the boxier the vessel. For round bilge a block of 0.32 is common; 0.34 for double chine craft; and 0.38 for single chine types.

Body plan This is also called the sectional view. The half sections of the vessel (sections on one side of the centreline only) are plotted on a centreline; usually that of the 'midships section (qv).

Bulwarks Continuation of the vessel's sides above the main deck. They may be continued at the same slope; vertically; or with some tumblehome (qv).

Buttocks Longitudinal, vertical slices through the hull parallel to the fore and aft centreline and at some specified distances from that line.

Camber The curvature or 'round-down' given to a deck such that it is higher in the centre than at the sides, principally to stiffen the deck. On small craft it also allows greater headroom below with less visual impact than raising the cabin sides. The camber curve is commonly the arc of a very large circle but parabolic curves can be substituted.

Centre of buoyancy (lcb) The centre of area of the immersed volume of the vessel whose position is specified longitudinally by the lcb and vertically by the vertical centre of buoyancy (vcb).

Centre of gravity (lcg) Overall centre of weight of the vessel including engines, fuel tanks, anchors etc. The lcg must lie in the same line as the lcb if the vessel is to trim correctly. The vcg (vertical centre of gravity) is also found by calculation when it is used, principally, in stability calculations.

Chine An abrupt change of shape between a boat's sides and bottom is called a chine. It occurs mainly on fast motor boats and is intended to throw water outwards as it climbs up the bottom at speed so that it does not wet the sides and cause added wetted surface (qv). It also makes for a craft that is easy to build from sheet materials such as ply or steel.

Curve of areas The areas of the immersed sections at various positions along the vessel's length are plotted out from the longitudinal centreline and a curve then drawn through these spots. The area under the curve represents the volume of displacement and its longitudinal centre of area will be at the same point as the lcb of the hull.

Deadrise Also called 'rise of floor' is the angle the bottom makes with the horizontal at the vertical centreline at some specified position. Thus the deadrise at the transom, say, is likely to be less than the deadrise at 'midships.

Diagonals Longitudinal slices through the hull set at an angle to the centreline are called diagonals. They are used mainly for fairing up the lines plan drawing and supplement the buttocks and waterlines used for the same purpose. The angle at which the diagonal is set and the point on the centreline from which it is drawn are given.

Displacement This is given as a weight or volume and is that weight or volume of water displaced by the vessel. This must equal the physical weight of the vessel itself for it to float at its designed waterline.

Effort, centre of (CE) The centre of area of the sail plan as a whole.

Flare The outwards curve of a hull's sides above the waterline. It is intended to deflect water outwards which would otherwise be blown aboard and thus promotes dryness. It also increases buoyancy as opposed to craft that might have plumb sides, and so helps reduce pitching.

Freeboard The vertical distance between the waterline and the top of the deck at side.

Gunwale The uppermost longitudinal strength member on a timber boat, and the one to which the deck is fastened at the deck side. It is also called 'the beam shelf' which is good description of its positioning.

Hull speed The speed a vessel reaches when $V/\sqrt{L} = 1.3$ or 1.4 which is the practical maximum for most sailing craft. A boat 25 ft long on the waterline would reach this at a speed of $V = 1.3$ or $1.4 \times \sqrt{25}$. That is, at 6.5 to 7 knots.

Lateral plane coefficient The ratio of the area of the underwater profile, including rudder, but excluding the centreboard, and the circumscribing rectangle. That is, the waterline length multiplied by maximum draught.

Lateral resistance; centre of (CLR) The centre of area of the underwater hull viewed in profile.

Lever As applied to displacement or weight calculations this is the distance between a fixed point and the centre of area or weight.

Lines plan The shape of a boat's hull shown in three planes or views: profile; plan (looking down on the craft); and sectional (called the body plan). Normally only half-sections are drawn, ie sections on one side of the centreline.

Midships The transverse section sited half way along the lwl.

Offsets A dimensioned guide of the lines plan. It gives, for instance, heights above and below lwl of the deck at side, chine, and buttocks; half-breadths from centreline of deck, chine and waterlines (and rabbet line on wooden boats); as well as dimensions from centreline down the various diagonals.

Planing A boat is said to be planing when dynamic lift starts to play its part and gradually take over from simple buoyant reaction. That will be at about a speed/length ratio of 3 to 3.5. On a 25 ft waterline craft this would imply a speed of 15 to 17.5 knots. When planing, a suitable hull form with a chine will be running with the body below the chine wetted but sides and transom running dry.

Prismatic coefficient The ratio of the immersed hull volume to the area of the 'midships section multiplied by waterline length. This gives an indication of the longitudinal distribution of displacement. A fine coefficient suggests that displacement is concentrated around 'midships with fine ends. A full coefficient implies just the opposite; a fine 'midships section and full ends. The coefficient is $\dfrac{\text{Disp.} \times 35}{L \times A_m}$ where L is waterline length and A_m is the area of the 'midships section.

Resistance It takes some power to drag a boat through the water at some given speed, and this figure is found either by practical experiment or, in the initial stages, by a towing tank, where a model of the craft will be towed along at its scale speed to see what resistance has to be overcome to achieve the velocity. Eventually this resistance, given first in lb, is translated into an effective horse power and then into the useable bhp (brake horsepower) figure.

Speed/length ratio Speed in knots divided by the square root of the waterline length. Thus, $\dfrac{V}{\sqrt{L}}$.

Spray rails Longitudinal strakes running along the bottom to deflect water away from the bottom area above the rail thus reducing wetted surface. Rails may also add a certain amount of lift and stiffen the boat's bottom structure.

Tumblehome The inwards slope or curvature of the hull above the waterline; and the inwards slope of the cabin side or bulwark. The opposite of flare.

Waterlines Horizontal, longitudinal slices through the hull. On a lines plane they appear as parallel straight lines at specified distances apart in profile, and on the plan view as curved lines.

Wetted surface Any part of a vessel's hull, including such items as propeller shafts, rudders and so on that is in contact with the water or heavy spray is counted as wetted surface. The object of a chine or spray rails, or both, is to deflect water or spray away from the bottom or sides and thus reduce the area of wetted surface and thus the power absorbed in driving through it.

Index

Bold numbers denote Glossary entry.